THE ANTICHRIST CHRONICLES

WHAT PROPHECY TEACHERS AREN'T TELLING YOU!

STEVE WOHLBERG

Texas Media Center
P.O. Box 330489
Fort Worth, TX 76163

Edited by B. Russell Holt
Designed by Steve Lanto
Cover design and inside art by Gary Will

Copyright © 2001 by Steve Wohlberg

Published by Texas Media Center
Printed in the United States of America

Unless otherwise credited, all Scripture quotations are
from the New King James Version of the Bible.

ISBN 0-8163-1908-1

01 02 03 04 05 • 6 5 4 3 2 1

Contents

Thank You!

I want to express my deepest appreciation to all my friends at the Texas Media Center for their hard work in making *The Antichrist Chronicles* into a television series. I look forward to seeing you all in the eternal kingdom of our Lord and Savior Jesus Christ.

Author's Introduction

On September 11, 2001, terrorist hijackers took over two U.S. planes and crashed them into the center of the world's most influential financial district—the twin towers of the World Trade Center in New York City—killing thousands of innocent people. Within minutes, another plane rammed into the heart of America's military intelligence—the Pentagon in Washington D.C. Trading ceased on the New York Stock Exchange. All U.S. airports shut down. News agencies around the globe tuned into the crisis. When President Bush proclaimed, "America is at war!" many prophecy-minded Christians wondered, "Is this the beginning of the end?"

Ten days later, on September 21, Americans poured into theaters for the opening release of the apocalyptic Christian film *Megiddo* to watch its portrayal of the biblical battle of Armageddon.

A few weeks later, on October 30, thousands stood in long lines at Christian bookstores to purchase *Desecration,* the ninth book in the best-selling *Left Behind* series. Both *Megiddo* and *Desecration* swirl around a similar theme—ancient prophecies, Earth's final crisis, an evil Antichrist, and an upcoming battle of Armageddon.

The Bible certainly does predict a coming global crisis. The book of Daniel says, " 'There shall be a time of trouble, such as never was since there was a nation even to that same time' " (Daniel 12:1). We are also informed that when the end finally comes, it will hit unexpectedly. Paul wrote, "When they say, 'Peace and Safety!' then sudden destruction comes upon them" (1 Thessalonians 5:3). And what about the concept of a sinister Antichrist—is such an idea fact or fiction? If we believe the Bible, the answer is, "It's fact," for the last book of God's Word declares, "And all the world marveled and followed the beast" (Revelation 13:3).

But let me clarify something. When most Bible prophecy teachers today talk about the end times, they have a very definite sequence of events in mind. Even though our times may be traumatic, most prophecy teachers believe that *before things get really bad and before the Antichrist shows up,* God will remove His church from Earth to heaven in an event called the Rapture. Thus the prophetic time-table is suggested to be as follows: *First* the Rapture, *then* the Antichrist, *then* Earth's final crisis, *then* Armageddon. Apocalyptic films such as *A Thief in the Night, Revelation, Tribulation,* and *Judgment,* in addition to best-selling books such as *Left Behind* and *Desecration*—all present this perspective. This sequence is now being taught on the radio, on television, in seminaries, on the Internet, and at Bible prophecy conferences. This is why even though such events as the destruction of the World Trade Center are frightening and terrible, Christians are still being comforted by the thought that they will be taken to heaven in the Rapture before Earth's last struggle—before the time of Antichrist.

In the light of recent global events and the seriousness of our times, there are some things you need to know. Not only was the week of September 11, "The week that America changed" (*Newsweek,* Sept. 21, 2001), but interpretations about prophecy *have also changed.* It's amazing to realize that it wasn't too long ago when the majority of prophecy-minded Christians—including Baptists, Methodists, Lutherans, Presbyterians, Reformed, Congregationalist, and Mennonite— interpreted God's ancient prophecies quite differently. Instead of believing in an Antichrist to come after the Rapture, they were convinced they were struggling against *a present Antichrist.* And for these Christians, this Antichrist was just as real as our current battle against modern terrorists. As you read this book, you will discover unquestionable proof behind this statement.

Before we delve deeper into this controversial topic, I want to say that I respect the God-given rights of every human being, whether they are Muslim, Jew, Protestant, Catholic, Hindu, or atheist. Every person should be treated with love, kindness, and respect, no matter what his or her beliefs or preferences. "Liberty and justice for all," is our national ideal. "God bless America!" is the desire of my heart. As a Jewish Christian, I also believe that Jesus Christ is the Savior of the world (1 John 4:14). Two thousand years ago, on a lonely hill outside Jerusalem, "Christ died for our sins" (1 Corinthians 15:3). At this very moment, Jesus longs to love, forgive, heal, and save every one of us by His grace (John 3:16; Ephesians 2:8). But when it comes to Bible prophecy, the truth must be told. Paul once said to a group of believers, "I have not shunned to declare to you the whole counsel of God" (Acts 20:27).

You will not find this book to be "politically correct," yet I hope for a fair, honest, and objective hearing. What you are about to read is very powerful, shocking, and yet totally biblical. I invite you to take out your personal copy of God's Book and see for yourself. Welcome to *The Antichrist Chronicles*. You are about to discover what prophecy teachers, although sincere, are simply not telling you.

CHAPTER 1

ANTICHRIST
IN THE BIBLE

When most Christians today think about the Antichrist, they usually think of only one highly intelligent, super-sinister Evil Person who will appear after the Rapture. *Left Behind: The Movie* calls him Nicolae Carpathia. In the end-time film series—*Apocalypse, Revelation, Tribulation,* and *Judgment*—his name is Franco Macalousso. With a creative twist going beyond similar movies, *Megiddo: Omega Code 2* portrays him (Stone Alexander) from boyhood on up, and even has him falling in love—until he reveals his true colors as the ultra-wicked incarnation of Satan himself.

What does the Holy Bible really teach about this hot subject? Let's find out. The word "antichrist," or "antichrists," is found only five

9

times in God's Word, and all of these references are found in only two small books right before Revelation, the last book of the Bible. The two little books are called 1 and 2 John. The exact verses are 1 John 2:18, 22; 4:3; and 2 John 7. When we read these verses and a few others surrounding them, this is what we find:

The early Christians had heard that antichrist was coming (1 John 2:18).

Even now there are many antichrists (1 John 2:18).

This is evidence that the last time has come (1 John 2:18).

These many antichrists come from *inside* of the Church (1 John 2:19).

Anyone who denies the Father and the Son is antichrist (1 John 2:22).

These antichrists are trying to seduce us away from Jesus Christ (1 John 2:26).

There is a spirit of antichrist (1 John 4:3).

The spirit of antichrist denies that Jesus Christ has come in the flesh (1 John 4:3).

The spirit of antichrist is already in the world (1 John 4:3).

True Christians must overcome every form of antichrist (1 John 4:4).

The spirit of antichrist is also the spirit of error (1 John 4:6).

There are many deceivers and antichrists in the world (2 John 7).

To overcome these antichrists, we must abide in the doctrine of Christ (2 John 9).

After an objective look, what have we discovered? Do any of these verses describe a solitary Mr. Sin who shows up only after we're gone? Definitely not! The Word describes not just one, *but many antichrists*. And according to 1 John 2:19, these many antichrists rise up from among "us," which means *from inside of the Christian church!* They are subtle, deceptive, and at war with true Christians. They may profess a certain faith in Christ, yet they actually deny the Father and the Son (1 John 2:22, 26). There is also a "spirit of antichrist," called the spirit of error, that is now in the world (1 John 4:3). According to the Bible, one of the goals of these many antichrists and of the spirit of antichrist is to deceive Christians regarding Jesus Christ and the true doctrine of Christ (2 John 7, 9). Just as America is now at war with terrorists, even so must genuine Christians do battle with these spiritual enemies of truth and overcome them in the strength of God (1 John 4:4).

This is everything God's Word actually says about "antichrist," "antichrists," and "the spirit of antichrist." Now don't miss this point. None of these passages point toward a single, solitary "Bad

Guy" like Nicolae Carpathia, Stone Alexander, or Franco Macalousso who shows up only after we're gone. In fact, the truth is quite different. In reality, all these passages refer to many seductive and deceiving elements which are *here now* and which true Christians must face and overcome.

It's true that God's Book does contain other prophecies about the mysterious emergence of an evil "little horn" (Daniel 7:8) a dreadful "beast" (Revelation 13:1), and a coming "man of sin" (2 Thessalonians 2:3). It's primarily these other prophecies that are now being used to support the idea of a single, future, evil Antichrist who will rise up *outside* of Christianity after the Rapture. Yet consider this. The definite trend of the Bible's literal "antichrist" passages clearly points to things that are here now and which true Christians must face and overcome. So why would its other "antichrist" prophecies suddenly reverse this trend and apply to things that Christians will *not face* because they will first vanish in the Rapture?

A few years ago I held a prophecy seminar in Corinth, Mississippi. En route by plane, I finally landed in Memphis, Tennessee. After picking up my rental car, I asked for directions to Corinth. Handing me a map, the attendant said calmly, "Get on I-55 and head south. You'll get there by and by." I had no reason to doubt. So, trustingly, I was soon rolling down Interstate 55. But after twenty minutes or so, a still, small voice started impressing my conscience to check the map for myself. At first, I ignored the voice. Finally, I reached over and took a look. To my amazement, I discovered that I-55 was heading straight south to Jackson, Mississippi, while Corinth was dead east! I turned around, went back to Memphis, got on the right road, and finally made it to my seminar.

The lesson I learned was this: No matter how much I may trust someone who gives me directions, I must always check the map for myself. Friend, the same thing applies to the subject of the Antichrist. We may trust that today's much-respected prophecy teachers know their stuff and won't lead us astray, but in the final analysis, we must look at God's map (the Bible) for ourselves. And so far, as we have done this, we have seen that all of the Word's clear "antichrist" statements definitely apply to *deceptive elements inside of Christianity* that we must face and overcome. But most best-selling books and thrilling apocalyptic movies don't tell us this. As you continue down the Antichrist Chronicles highway, checking God's map closely and listening for His voice, you will discover many other things that prophecy teachers aren't telling you!

CHAPTER 2

What the majority of people think is often wrong. People thought the *Titanic* was unsinkable, yet she sank like lead. Many believed the infamous Y2K computer glitch would result in a global economic meltdown as the world's clocks ticked over to the year 2000. Yet January 1 arrived with hardly a hiccup. Star-struck lovers race to the marriage altar fully expecting a lifetime of bliss, yet after a few short days reality sometimes hits like a boxer's glove to the nose. It's obvious isn't it? What we humans *think* will happen often fails to occur.

When it comes to the arena of Bible prophecy, is it possible that major mistakes are also being made? At this very moment, millions of Christians fully expect to vanish in the Rapture before the Antichrist arrives. Thus the idea is—*First* the Rapture, *then* the Antichrist. This sequence is being taught all around the world in books, magazines, and seminars, on radio, television, and the Internet. Yet will it really happen this way? The answer, of course, is in the Bible.

The most quoted passage about the Rapture is found in 1 Thessalonians 4:17. Paul wrote that believers will be someday be "caught up." Then in 2 Thessalonians 2 Paul wrote about the coming of something or someone that is clearly Antichrist. The question we wish to ask is this: What did Paul really teach about the sequence of events? Did he say the church would be "caught up" *before* Antichrist comes or will Antichrist come *first,* before the Rapture? Amazingly, Paul gives us a straight answer—and this answer is not what most people think!

In order to discover Paul's answer, we need to examine three key sections from his writings that greatly illuminate this topic. I have listed these sections below, along with a quick summary of what each is about:

1. 1 Thessalonians 4:16–5:3. The Day of the Lord when the church is caught up.
2. 2 Thessalonians 1:7-10. Further clarification about this Day of the Lord.
3. 2 Thessalonians 2:1-3. Insights about the arrival and nature of Antichrist.

When we are finished with this chapter, there will be no doubt as to which comes first—the Rapture or the arrival of the Antichrist.

1 Thessalonians 4:16–5:3

The Bible says, "For the Lord Himself will descend from heaven with a shout, with the voice of an archangel, and with the trumpet of God. And the dead in Christ will rise first. Then we who are alive and remain shall be caught up together with them in the clouds to meet the Lord in the air. And thus we shall always be with the Lord. Therefore comfort one another with these words. But concerning the times and seasons, brethren, you have no need that I should write to you. For you yourselves know perfectly that the day of the Lord so comes as a thief in the night. For when they say, 'Peace and safety!' then sudden destruction comes upon them, as labor pains upon a pregnant woman. And they shall not escape" (1 Thessalonians 4:16-5:3).

You don't need a college degree to understand these words! Paul clearly wrote that Jesus Christ is coming down from heaven with a shout, a voice, and the trumpet of God. When He does, the dead in Christ will rise, and then all of God's children will be "caught up" to meet the Lord in the sky. This great "day of the Lord" will come unexpectedly, like a thief in the night, and when it does, those who are not ready will be suddenly destroyed by His return. Thus there are only two options: People will be caught up or suddenly destroyed. It's that simple.

It's important to realize that Paul wrote these words nearly two thousand years ago to a group of Christians who lived in a city called Thessalonica, in northern Greece. When these Christians first read Paul's letter, they became very excited about the return of Christ. In fact, some could hardly wait. But soon a definite problem developed. Evidently, Satan saw their excitement and decided to bring in a false idea—an extreme view. It was largely because of this problem that Paul decided to write his second letter to the same church. What was this false idea? Primarily, it was the mistaken concept that the Day of Christ was about to come very "soon," was "at hand," or had even "already come" in some sort of secret, spiritual way (see 2 Thessalonians 2:2, KJV; NKJV). A few church members even quit their jobs and withdrew from normal living (see 2 Thessalonians 3:10-12). Again, this is one of the main reasons Paul decided to write his second letter.

2 Thessalonians 1:7-10

Paul's second letter to Thessalonian Christians was also addressed to "the church of the Thessalonians" (2 Thessalonians 1:1). In Chapter 1, verses 7-10, he tackled head on the false idea that the Day of Christ had *already come* in some sort of secret, spiritual way. He began by pointing forward to the time "when the Lord Jesus is revealed from heaven" (verse 7). These words unmistakably parallel his previous description in his first letter of the great day when "the Lord Himself shall descend from heaven" (1 Thessalonians 4:16). If one simply puts both sentences side by side, it is clear that Paul is writing about the same event. One description is near the end of his first letter, and the other is at the beginning of his second letter. At the start of his second letter, Paul makes two points extremely clear: (1) This Day of Christ has *not* already come; and (2) When it hits, it will be *anything but secret!*

Here's the proof. Paul wrote, "You who are troubled, rest with us when the Lord Jesus is revealed from heaven with His mighty angels, in flaming fire taking vengeance on those who do not know God, and on those who do not obey the gospel of our Lord Jesus Christ. These shall be punished with everlasting destruction from the presence of the Lord and from the glory of His power, when He comes, in that Day, to be glorified in His saints and to be admired among all those who believe, because our testimony among you was believed" (2 Thessalonians 1:7-10). These words perfectly parallel what Paul previously wrote in 1 Thessalonians 4:16–5:3. Yet here Paul adds the additional clarification that this return of Jesus will be with mighty angels and with flames of fire! How awesome! Thus Paul dealt a death-blow to the mistaken notion that the Day of Christ had already come. And just as in his first letter, Paul said that those who are not ready for this return would experience "destruction," even "everlasting destruction." In other words, they will be lost forever.

2 Thessalonians 2:1-3

At the beginning of *The Antichrist Chronicles,* we not only showed from the Bible that the word *antichrist* is used only in 1 and 2 John, but also that there are really "many antichrists" (1 John 2:18). In 2 Thessalonians 2, even though Paul doesn't use the word *antichrist,* he is plainly talking about someone or something that is clearly evil and anti-Christian. Paul calls him, or it, "the man of sin" (verse 3), "the son of perdition" (verse 3), "the mystery of lawlessness" (verse 7), and "that Wicked" (verse 8, KJV). Most prophecy scholars today identify this someone or something as *the Antichrist.*

I agree. The question now to be settled is this: Does this Antichrist come *after* the Church is caught up, as is commonly taught in books such as *Left Behind* and such thrilling apocalyptic movies as *A Thief in the Night* or does he come *first,* before the church is gathered to Jesus Christ? Is it possible to know for sure? Let's find out.

Paul wrote, "Now, brethren, concerning the coming of our Lord Jesus Christ and our gathering together to Him [a parallel to 1 Thessalonians 4:17], we ask you, not to be soon shaken in mind or troubled, either by spirit or by word or by letter, as if from us, as though the day of Christ had come. Let no man deceive you by any means; for that Day will not come unless the falling away comes first, and the man of sin is revealed, the son of perdition" (2 Thessalonians 2:1-3).

Do you realize what you just read? Paul's words are nothing short of cataclysmic when it comes to the issue of which comes first, the Rapture or the Antichrist. Here is a brief and simple summary:

Verse 1: Paul wrote about "the coming of our Lord Jesus Christ and our gathering together to Him." Our gathering to Jesus is the same thing as our being "caught up" to meet Him in the sky (1 Thessalonians 4:17). It's obvious that this gathering or catching up of God's church occurs at the return of Jesus Christ.

Verse 2: Here Paul plainly addressed the distortion. He urged the Thessalonians not to be "soon shaken," or "troubled," by false influences which were teaching that "the Day of Christ *had come,*" or, as the King James Version puts it, that it was "at hand" in the first century.

Verse 3: Paul then clarified that "that Day [when Jesus comes to gather us] shall not come except there come a falling away *first,* and that man of sin be revealed, the son of perdition." Did you catch that? Are you awake? Do you see it?

In verse 3, the Bible is amazingly clear. Contrary to popular opinion, Paul said the falling away and the rise of the Antichrist must come *first,* before the church is "caught up," or gathered to Jesus Christ (verse 1). But there is more. Are you ready for it? Paul directly and most specifically warns us *not to be deceived* about this very thing! Evidently Satan will really work hard to trick us in this exact area.

When we simply put the pieces together, it becomes superclear that when Jesus Christ comes down from heaven to catch up His church (1 Thessalonians 4:16, 17), He is coming with mighty angels and in flaming fire (2 Thessalonians 1:7, 8). How awesome! This completely blows away any *secret coming* idea. But for those early Thessalonians, that tremendous day was not just a few inches around the corner. Why wasn't it? Because the falling away must come *first* and the Antichrist must be revealed.

Yes, Jesus Christ will surely come to gather His children.

But according to God's eternal Word, the Antichrist must come first.

I know many today think differently. But remember—many also *thought* the *Titanic* was unsinkable!

CHAPTER 3

Millions of Christians are now being taught that the Antichrist will be some evil person who will rise into power *outside* of Christianity *after* the Rapture. But think with me for a moment. What if, somehow, this idea is actually a horrible mistake? What if the Antichrist rises up *inside* of Christianity *before* the Church is caught up to Christ? Because few would be looking for an Antichrist within, can you imagine what kind of harm he could do? Hold onto your seats, for you are about to discover that the apostle Paul himself taught this very thing.

Paul wrote, "Let no one deceive you by any means; for that Day [the day when Jesus returns to gather us] will not come unless the *falling away* comes first, and the man of sin is revealed, the son of perdition" (2 Thessalonians 2:3, italics supplied). Almost everyone agrees that these words predict the rise of the Antichrist. But what many have missed is that Paul is describing an Antichrist that comes as a result of "the falling away." What does this mean? The Greek word Paul used for "the falling away," is *apostasia,* which literally means *an apostasy* or departure from Jesus Christ *inside* the Christian church.

To illustrate the connection between "the falling away," and the rising up of the Antichrist, imagine a boy who climbs a tree, stands on a branch, loses his footing, and then "falls away." After hitting his head on the ground, a large bump starts growing on his head. Surely you can see the simple connection between the boy's "falling away" from the branch and the rising up of the bump. It's the same with the falling away and the rising up of the Antichrist. And as we shall see, this "falling away" unquestionably takes place *inside* the church.

In the first century, the Christian church remained relatively pure from heresy, false doctrine, and open sin. But with His cosmic perspective, God saw that a change would come, and He revealed this sober reality to the writers of the New Testament. A brief survey of the following Bible passages show plainly that an apostasy, departure, or "falling away" from Jesus Christ was predicted to occur *inside* of Christianity. We might call this "The Big Detour."

1. Acts 20. Paul told "the elders of the church" of Ephesus (verse 17) that soon many false Christian leaders would rise up from *among themselves* to "draw away the disciples" after them (verse 30). He was so burdened about this coming apostasy that he warned the church "night and day with tears" (verse 31).

2. 1 Timothy 4. The Holy Spirit clearly warned that "some will depart from the faith, giving heed to deceiving spirits and doctrines of demons" (verse 1). Here again is a predicted departure from the faith taking place *inside* the church.

3. 2 Timothy 4. Paul declared that a time would come when many in the church "will not endure sound doctrine, but according to their own desires, because they have itching ears, they will heap up for themselves teachers; and they will turn their ears away from the truth, and be turned aside to fables" (verses 3, 4). Friend, there is no doubt about it. These words point toward *an apostasy in the church* that will lead professed Christians to turn away from the truth to fables.

4. 2 Peter 2. Peter told the early believers that soon "there will be false teachers *among you*" (verse 1). "Among you" means inside the church.

5. Jude. After urging believers to contend earnestly for the original faith, Jude warned that "certain men" had already "crept in unnoticed" among them (verse 4).

6. Revelation 2. Jesus Christ Himself sadly told His early followers in the church of Ephesus, "Nevertheless, I have this against you, that you have left your first love. Remember therefore from where you have fallen; repent and do the first works" (verses 4, 5). These words are so clear! Many Christians in the early church of Ephesus were *falling away* from their initial love for Jesus Christ, who died for them.

Thus we see Paul, Peter, Jude, and Jesus Christ all deeply concerned about "the falling away," which means *an apostasy*, occurring inside the Christian church. We might compare this apostasy to a disease entering a portion of a human body. As a result, a malignant cancer finally develops. The shocking reality is that God's Word has predicted that a similar diseaselike condition would eventually overtake a large portion of Christianity. And according to 2 Thessalonians 2, as a direct result of this disease, a diabolical spiritual cancer would begin to rise up.

Paul called this cancer, "the mystery of lawlessness" (2 Thessalonians 2:7).

We call him Antichrist.

CHAPTER 4

ANTICHRIST
IS THE SON OF PERDITION

The apostle Paul warned, "Let no one deceive you by any means; for that Day [the day when Jesus Christ returns to gather us] shall not come unless the falling away comes first, and the man of sin is revealed, *the son of perdition*" (2 Thessalonians 2:3, italics supplied). Here Paul called the Antichrist, "the son of perdition."

Believe it or not, this phrase—the son of perdition—is actually like a secret password to hidden knowledge. Our society is now making a full use of similar passwords, passphrases, or passcodes. When you call your bank with an inquiry about your account, the attendant usually asks, "What's your mothers maiden name?" Or, "What's your Social Security number?" Or simply,

"What's your password?" The same thing happens on the Internet when a person attempts to access his bank account, phone account, or stock account. After typing in the correct phrase on the keyboard, the person may "Enter" and access his account.

As we are about to see, the biblical phrase "the son of perdition" also has certain passwordlike qualities. In essence, those four words are like a special code. Once we understand their meaning, we are enabled to "Enter" into an understanding of *the true nature of Antichrist.*

This exact phrase, "the son of perdition," occurs only twice in the entire New Testament. One of these is 2 Thessalonians 2:3 referring to the Antichrist. What about the other occurance? To whom did it apply and what spiritual lesson can we learn from this? The only other place this phrase is used in the Bible is John 17:12 when Jesus Christ applied it to one of His own disciples. You should be able to guess which one. That's right. It was Judas Iscariot, His betrayer.

Judas was one of the twelve disciples of Jesus Christ. After being chosen by the Lord, he became part of Christ's inner circle (Luke 6:13-16). Amazingly, Judas even received the power of God (Matthew 10:1-4). But in spite of his tremendous privileges, he finally fell away from his Savior (Acts 1:25).

27

The Bible says, "Then Satan entered Judas surnamed Iscariot, who was numbered among the twelve" (Luke 22:3). What a scary verse! Try to imagine it. Here's a disciple of Jesus Christ who held an honored position as one of the Twelve. He even carried the moneybag. But as Judas opened his heart to the enemy, Satan slipped in and completely took over. Judas was still a professed Christian, but now he had a devil inside! Is this what Antichrist will be like?

On the last night before His final agony, Jesus Christ met with His little band of followers in an upper room somewhere inside Jerusalem. This was an intimate, private gathering for only His closest friends. As they gathered for the Passover meal, Judas quietly took his seat with the other eleven disciples (Luke 22:14). After Jesus passed around the bread and the juice, Judas silently sipped from his cup (Luke 22:19, 20). When the supper was over, Jesus sadly whispered to His friends, " 'Behold, the hand of My betrayer is with Me on the table' " (Luke 22:21). A few minutes later, Judas stepped out into the night to finalize his infamous deal with the rulers of Israel. An ancient word was fulfilled, "Even my own familiar friend in whom I trusted, Who ate my bread, Has lifted up his heel against me" (Psalm 41:9). How terrible, to be betrayed by *a friend!*

A few hours later, in the Garden of Gethsemane, Judas led the chief priests and a mob of Roman soldiers to Christ's secret place of prayer. Approaching the Savior, Judas said, "Hail master, and kissed him" (Matthew 26:49, KJV). Oh, what a kiss was this! Was it a sign of true affection? No! It was a kiss of death! What's really happening here? I'll tell you. There was Lucifer himself working through the kiss of a professed Christian in a satanically orchestrated plot against the Son of God! If you think about it, *this is Anti-Christ* in its highest and most sinister form!

To all appearances, on the outside, Judas Iscariot was a faithful apostle of Jesus. With his lips he even called Christ his master, but his foul breath was full of satanic venom. By this time, Judas was fully " 'a devil' " (John 6:70). Now don't miss this point: he was a *Christian* devil—a channel for Satan who was hiding behind *a Christian mask*. Behold the ultimate deception! What could be worse than Satan working through a highly honored Christian, through words of loyalty, through an affectionate kiss? And what highly significant phrase did Jesus finally use to describe this unusual professing Christian-kissing-satanic combination? Our Lord called Judas, " *'the son of perdition'* " (John 17:12).

This is what Paul called *the Antichrist* (2 Thessalonians 2:3)! In so doing, He is actually revealing secret, vital, inside information. As we approach our biblical monitors and type in this passphrase—THE SON OF PERDITION—the words are "Accepted" and we are enabled to "Enter" into a true understanding of the real nature of Antichrist. Instead of being an obviously evil, openly anti-Christian person who will rise from *outside* of the church, the real Antichrist will be Judas-like. In other words, he will come from the inner circle. On the surface, he will look like a true follower of Jesus Christ, a "familiar friend" (Psalm 41:9). He will even profess love for and loyalty to the Savior. Yet the devil will be there in secret, working with ingenious subtlety, to betray the Son of God with a kiss.

CHAPTER 5

ANTICHRIST
IS THE MAN OF SIN

Paul called the Antichrist, "the man of sin" (2 Thessalonians 2:3). It is primarily because of this single verse that millions have concluded that the Antichrist will be a single individual—one wicked man. Kids who read the popular *Left Behind* books sometimes call him the Evil Dude. Apocalyptic Christian films such as *The Omega Code, Image of the Beast, Tribulation, Judgment,* and *Megiddo,* reflect the same idea. Is it true? Will there be only one super-sinister "Bad Guy" who becomes *the* Antichrist—an Osama bin Laden Number 2? Is this what Paul really meant?

In Chapter 1 of *The Antichrist Chronicles,* we discovered that John wrote about "many antichrists" (1 John 2:18) and a "spirit of antichrist" (1 John

4:3, KJV). He also revealed that any person who denies "the doctrine of Christ" (2 John 9) is "a deceiver and *an antichrist*" (2 John 7, italics supplied). Therefore the idea of only one "Mr. Sinister" as *the* Antichrist fails the biblical test.

Truth can afford to be fair. It has nothing to hide and is willing to examine every iota of evidence. So what did Paul mean when he wrote about "the man of sin"? First, Paul uses other phrases to describe this same Antichrist—such terms as "the son of perdition," (verse 3), "the mystery of lawlessness" (verse 7), and "that Wicked" (verse 8, KJV). In Daniel's parallel prophecy, this very same abominable horror is also called a little "horn" (Daniel 7:8); and in the book of Revelation it is labeled "the beast" (Revelation 13:2). Almost everyone agrees that all of these words and phrases apply to the same thing. The big question is: Do all these terms apply to only one evil individual who shows up after the Rapture, as is commonly taught, or do they point to something much wider and deeper—to something most prophecy teachers aren't telling you about?

Notice carefully, Daniel did not say the little horn would *be* a man, but rather that it would have "eyes *like* the eyes of a man" (Daniel 7:8, italics supplied). In the book of Revelation, the same horn is called "the beast." But how does Daniel 7 *define* a beast? There is no need to guess. In Daniel 7, an angelic interpreter declared, "The fourth beast shall be a fourth kingdom on earth" (verse 7). Presto! So what is a beast? A man? A giant computer? No. A beast is *a kingdom!* That's what God's Word says.

Let's go back to Paul's prophecy. A careful study of 2 Thessalonians 2 actually reveals the utter impossibility of "the man of sin" applying to only a single evil person who appears only after the Rapture. One reason is because Paul said that in his own time "the mystery of lawlessness [was] already at work" (verse 7). Thus this mysterious Antichrist was already beginning to work in the first century. Paul is also very emphatic that this "mystery" would continue all the way down to the very Second Coming of Jesus Christ (verse 8). Put the pieces together. How could this refer to only one man? He would have to be 2,000 years old!

Here's an important question. Did Paul ever use this expression, "the man," in any of his other writings in such a way that it does *not* refer to only one man? Yes. Paul wrote, "All Scripture is given by inspiration of God, and is profitable for doctrine, for reproof, for correction, for instruction in righteousness, that *the man* of God may be complete, thoroughly equipped for every good work" (2 Timothy 3:15, 16, italics supplied). Do you see it? Does this phrase, "the man of God," refer to one single holy man who might have a name like Joe or Bill or Frank? Of course not! Instead, this phrase refers to a succession of godly men throughout history who become "complete" or "perfect" (verse 17, KJV) through the Word of God.

In Romans 13, Paul also used the phrase "*the minister* of God" (verse 4, KJV, italics supplied) to refer to all civil officers throughout history whom God uses to restrain evil. Therefore if we let Paul's own writings interpret themselves, his unique phrase, "the man of sin" (2 Thessalonians 2:3), need not apply to only one ultra-evil Antichrist person. Then what might it apply to? In the blazing light of 2 Timothy 3:17 and Romans 13:4, Paul's expression, "the man of sin," could properly apply to a historical succession of other men who follow tradition and sin above the pure Word of truth.

CHAPTER 6

ANTICHRIST
IN THE TEMPLE OF GOD

T he best-selling *Left Behind* series swirls completely around the topic of the Antichrist. Book 9 of these fictitious novels is called *Desecration—Antichrist Takes the Throne.* Of this book, released on October 30, 2001 with an initial print run of three million copies, the official *Left Behind* Web site declared, "In *Desecration,* Antichrist Nicolae Carpathia enters the temple in Jerusalem and declares himself God, leading the world to the brink of Armageddon." Thus the center of the storm is Jerusalem and the apex of the drama centers around Nicolae's abominable entrance into a rebuilt Jewish Temple.

The cornerstone Bible passage underlying the theology of *Desecration* and of countless other prophecy books that teach similar things is 2 Thessalonians 2:4. Describing the Antichrist, Paul wrote that he "opposes and exalts himself above all that is called God or that is worshiped, so that he sits as God in the temple of God, showing himself that he is God" (verse 4). Thus Antichrist will sit "in the temple of God." *Desecration* applies this to someone like Nicolae Carpathia who will one day enter a literal rebuilt temple in Jerusalem after the Rapture. The clear implication of this common interpretation is that 2 Thessalonians 2:4 has nothing to do with Christians today, nor has it had any relevance to the church for the past 2,000 years. Is this popular interpretation *really* what Paul had in mind? Let's take a closer look.

The Greek word that Paul used for "temple" in 2 Thessalonians 2:4 is *naos*. We've been following the safe principle of letting Paul interpret Paul, so let's see how he used this same Greek word in his other letters. Writing to "the church of God which is at Corinth" (1 Corinthians 1:2), Paul asked, "Do you not know that you are the temple [*naos*] of God and that the Spirit of God dwells in you?" (1 Corinthians 3:16). Here Paul applied the word *naos* to the church! He did the same thing in his letter to the Ephesians. Writing to "the saints who are in Ephesus" (Ephesians 1:1), Paul said they were all growing "into a holy temple [*naos*] in the Lord" (Ephesians 2:21). In fact, in all of his writings, every time Paul used the word *naos,* he *always applied* it to the Christian church and *never* to a rebuilt Israeli temple!

Consider this. When Jesus Christ died on Calvary, He put an end to all bloody animal sacrifices. When He cried out, " 'It is finished' " (John 19:30), that was it. From God's cosmic perspective, all earthly sacrifices were over because His Son had become the final Sacrifice (Hebrews 10:12). If the Jewish people ever do rebuild a temple in Jerusalem and restart bloody sacrifices, these would in themselves be a denial of Christ's sacrifice. Now think seriously: Could a rebuilt Jewish temple that denies Jesus Christ ever properly be called by Paul, "the temple *of God*"? Not in a million light years! Such a temple would not be *God's* temple, for it would be an open denial of His Son. The correct interpretation of 2 Thessalonians 2:4, based on Paul's own usage of the word *naos,* is that "the temple of God" *is the church.* The lesson for prophecy students is this— Antichrist, subtle and deceptive, *is predicted to enter Christianity.*

Antichrist will "sit" in the temple of God. This doesn't mean he will sit in a chair in some physical building. After Jesus ascended to heaven, He "sat down at the right hand of God" (Hebrews 10:12). Does this mean He's been sitting down for 2,000 years? Obviously not. When Christ returns, He will come "sitting at the right hand of the Power, and coming on the clouds of heaven" (Matthew 26:64). Does this mean He will return sitting on a fast-moving heavenly chair? No again! To sit means to sit in a position of authority. When George Bush was inaugurated as President of the United States on January 20, 2001, newspapers around the world referred to him as being officially "seated" in office. When Jesus Christ ascended to heaven to sit at the right hand of the Father, this means He was officially seated in office as our great High Priest in the sanctuary above (Hebrews 8:1, 2). He now has all authority in heaven and on earth (Matthew 28:18).

Then what is the meaning of the Antichrist sitting in the temple of God? A little reflection should make this clear. The shocking reality is that prophecy predicts that the Antichrist will one day usurp the legitimate authority of Jesus Christ by assuming an unauthorized position of power *inside the Christian church.* And thus, contrary to the best-selling book, *Desecration,* Paul's prediction about an evil Antichrist entering the temple of God has great relevance for Christians today.

CHAPTER 7

ANTICHRIST
AND THE RESTRAINER

In the 1800s there supposedly lived a man named Sherlock Holmes. His name has become famous as one of the greatest detectives of all time. According to mystery writer Sir Aurthur Conan Doyle, Mr. Holmes lived in a small apartment on Baker Street, in London, England. A museum exists there today to the delight of his fans. The living room, dining room, and bedroom have all been preserved—providing excellent footage for many Sherlock Holmes films. As the story goes, Sherlock often sat in his study with his good friend Dr. Watson, smoking his pipe, as they carefully pieced together bits of information to solve crimes.

In this chapter we wish to play the role of Sherlock Holmes by attempting to solve a most puzzling Bible mystery. The difficult question is: Who or what is the Restrainer of Antichrist? In 2 Thessalonians 2:5-8, Paul revealed the unique idea that in his day something or someone was restraining this horrendous development of evil. Once the restraint was removed, Antichrist would be revealed. Millions of Christians today are being taught that this Restrainer is the Holy Spirit inside the Christian church. According to this theory, once the church is removed from this world in the Rapture, then the Antichrist will appear. This interpretation once again confirms the concept in many minds that the Antichrist can come only *after* the church disappears.

Sherlock Holmes is purported to have said, "It is a capital mistake to theorize before one has data." So, let's examine the data. Paul told the early Thessalonians, "Do you not remember that when I was still with you I told you these things? And now you know what is restraining, that he may be revealed in his own time. For the mystery of lawlessness is already at work; only he who now restrains will do so until he is taken out of the way. And then the lawless one will be revealed" (2 Thessalonians 2:5-8).

To begin with, we must admit that Paul did not specify what was restraining the Antichrist. Nevertheless, the following three facts are clear:

1. Paul had previously "told" the Thessalonians what the Restrainer was (verse 5).
2. Thus the Thessalonians knew what it was (verse 6).
3. For some important reason, Paul did not identify in writing what it was.

Sherlock Holmes is also believed to have said, "Detection is, or should be, an exact science." As we ponder the evidence above, a significant detail surfaces. Because Paul plainly said he had "told" the Thessalonians what the Restrainer was, then this knowledge had obviously been given to the early church. So, as good detectives, what should we do next? It seems logical that we should first go back into the dusty records of ancient history in an attempt to discover what the early church might have written on this subject. Can't you just hear Mr. Holmes repeating his most classic line to Watson, "It's elementary, my dear Watson, elementary!" Yes, it is. So let's go back and find out.

Did the early Christians tell us later what they knew about this subject? Did they identify the Restrainer? The answer, surprisingly, is yes. Such early writers as Irenaeus, Tertullian, Chrysostom, Jerome, and Augustine all wrote about this topic. What did they say? They all said the Restrainer was *the civil power of the Roman*

Empire ruled by the Caesars. Notice carefully the following quotations:

"He who now hinders must hinder until he be taken out of the way. What obstacle is there but the Roman state; the falling away of which, by being scattered into ten kingdoms, shall introduce antichrist" (Tertullian *On the Resurrection,* Chapters 24, 25). Tertullian was a Christian in North Africa around A.D. 200.

" 'Only there is one that restraineth now, until he be taken out of the way,' that is, when the Roman Empire is taken out of the way, then he [Antichrist] shall come. And naturally. For as long as the fear of this empire lasts, no one will willingly exit himself, but when that is dissolved, he will attack the anarchy, and endeavor to seize upon the government both of man and of God" (John Chrysostom, *Sermon on 2 Thessalonians 2. Number 4*). Chrysostom was Bishop of Constantinople in A.D. 390.

"It is not absurd to believe that these words of the apostle, 'Only he who now holdeth, let him hold until he be taken out of the way,' refer to the Roman empire"

(Augustine, *The City of God,* Book 20, Chapter 19). Augustine was a Christian bishop in North Africa around A.D. 400.

Thus the historical evidence reveals that the early church believed the Roman Empire was restraining the Antichrist. Others have also recognized this fact. "We have the consenting testimony of the early Fathers, from Irenaeus, the disciple of St. John, down to Chrysostom and Jerome, to the effect that it [the Restrainer] was understood to be the imperial power ruling and residing at Rome" (Edward B. Elliot, *Commentary on the Apocalypse,* volume 3, p. 92.) The much-respected George Eldon Ladd also confirmed, "The traditional view has been that the restraining principle is the Roman Empire and the restrainer the Emperor. This view, or a modification of it, best fits into the Pauline theology" *(A Theology of the New Testament,* p. 560.)

When modern interpreters identify the Restrainer as the Holy Spirit inside the Christian church, we should recognize that this interpretation is not based on historical evidence. As Mr. Holmes said, "Detection is, or should be, an exact science," and it's simply not historically accurate to say that the Holy Spirit inside the church is the Restrainer. Unfortunately, this theory has now become one of the supporting pillars beneath the idea that the Rapture must come *before* Antichrist can show up. But we have already proven from 2 Thessalonians 2 itself that it's really the other way around! Paul emphatically said that Antichrist *must come first* (verse 3) before the church is gathered to Jesus Christ (verse 1)!

In addition to being directly told by Paul that the Restrainer of the Antichrist was the Roman Empire, there is an additional reason why the early church would have believed this. This reason may be found in the parallel prophecy of Daniel 7. Daniel's prophecy predicted the rise of four great beasts representing four successive world empires (verse 23). Those empires were the kingdoms of Babylon, Persia, Greece, and Rome. The fourth beast, which clearly was the Roman Empire, had ten horns (verse 7). After the ten horns would rise another "little horn"—the Antichrist (verse 8). The lesson is clear. After the fourth beast, that is, *after Rome fell,* then the Antichrist would rise up among the "ten horns" of Europe.

The early Thessalonians lived under the rule of Rome. Through understanding the prophecies, they knew that after Rome fell, the Antichrist would come. This helps explain why the early Christians (according to Tertullian) made it a habit to pray for the continuation of that very empire, even though it was persecuting them for their faith in Jesus Christ (see 2 Thessalonians

1:4). But wait a minute! Here's another important piece of data! The reality of this fierce Roman persecution against the early Christians provides a logical explanation as to why Paul only "told" the Thessalonians what the Restrainer was, rather than writing it down. The reason is simple. What if his letter had fallen into the hands of Roman officials? What if they had found out that these Christians expected their mighty empire to someday crash, being "taken out of the way" (verse 7)? The answer is obvious. They would have seen this as treason against Caesar and would have increased their persecution against the infant church. This explains why, instead of writing it down, Paul merely "told" them. Can't you see Sherlock's piercing eyes as he gathers information while smoking his pipe? "This is key data," he would surely whisper to Watson.

Paul wrote: "For the mystery of lawlessness is already at work, only he who now restrains will do so, until he is taken out of the way" (2 Thessalonians 2:7). Thus the Antichrist was "already" starting to work in Paul's time, yet he was restrained. Once the restrainer was removed, this monstrous evil would fully rise to power in Europe. In other words, once the Caesars went down, the Antichrist would rise up. H. Grattan Guinness, who has been called England's greatest Bible prophecy teacher, said it this way: "While the

Caesars held imperial power, it was impossible for the predicted antichrist to arise . . . on the fall of the Caesars he would arise" (*Romanism and the Reformation,* p. 105).

Here's a simple summary of the Biblical data found in 2 Thessalonians 2:

1. The Antichrist was already starting to work in Paul's day (verse 7).
2. But something was restraining this horrible development of evil (verses 5-7).
3. As soon as the restraint was removed, Antichrist would be revealed (verses 7, 8).
4. This Antichrist will continue until the visible return of Jesus Christ (verse 8).
5. Then Christ will destroy the Antichrist and gather His church (verses 1, 8).

Daniel wrote that after the fourth beast fell, the little horn would come (Daniel 7:7, 8). Paul said that after the Restrainer was taken out of the way, the Antichrist would be revealed (2 Thessalonians 2:7, 8). History records that the Roman Empire collapsed in A.D. 476. Is the Antichrist here now?

Sherlock Holmes would say, "It's elementary, my dear Watson, elementary!"

CHAPTER 8

ANTICHRIST
PROPHECIES SUMMARIZED

When I was a boy, I used to love super-complicated jigsaw puzzles. Hour after hour I would sit, ponder, and put in the pieces. As you can imagine, it was always exciting for me to see the last few pieces finally fit together. When the full image of a house, a car, or a lake completely emerged, I would happily call my mother and say, "There, I did it!" And she would smile approvingly.

The Bible's prophecies about the Antichrist are similar to a gigantic jigsaw puzzle. While it's important to carefully examine the individual pieces, it's really best to put them all together and look at whole thing. When we do, just like a developing photograph in a darkroom, the emerging picture becomes clearer and clearer. This is what we find.

Putting the pieces together from Daniel 7

1. Daniel dreamed of four great beasts representing four successive ancient world kingdoms (verse 23).

2. These kingdoms were the nations of Babylon, Persia, Greece, and Rome.

3. The fourth beast, representing the Roman Empire, had ten horns (verse 7) which represented the division of the western Roman Empire into ten smaller nations after A.D. 476 (the classic date for the fall of Rome).

4. Growing up "among" the ten horns (verse 8), and rising up immediately "after" them (verse 24), would be a little horn (verse 8) *which represents the Antichrist.*

5. This little horn would have "eyes like the eyes of a man" (verse 8), "a mouth speaking pompous words" (verse 8), and would make "war against the saints" (verse 21) in Christian history. This horn would ultimately continue until the end of the age (verses 21, 22).

Putting the pieces together from 2 Thessalonians 2

1. The Antichrist would rise as a result of a tremendous falling away (verse 3) in the church before Jesus Christ returns to gather the faithful (verse 1).

2. Paul called this Antichrist "the man of sin" (verse 3), "the son of perdition" (verse 3), "the mystery of lawlessness" (verse 7), and "that Wicked" (verse 8, KJV).

3. This "mystery of lawlessness" was already starting to work in Paul's day (verse 7), yet it was being restrained (verses 5-7) by the rule of the Caesars and the Roman Empire (see Chapter 7 of this book).

4. After the Restrainer was removed (Rome fell in A.D. 476), the Antichrist would be revealed (verses 7, 8).

5. This Antichrist would take his seat inside the temple of God (verse 4) which represents the Christian church (see 1 Corinthians 3:16).

6. This Antichrist will continue all the way until the highly visible and ultra-glorious return of Jesus Christ (verse 8).

7. Then Jesus Christ will destroy the Antichrist and gather His faithful people who have not "fallen away" from Him or from *the truth* of His Word (verses 1, 3, 8, 10-12)!

Putting the pieces together from Revelation 13

1. The Antichrist is also called "the beast" (verse 2).

2. This "beast" is the same thing as the "little horn" in Daniel 7.

3. Just like the little horn, this beast would have "a mouth speaking great things" (verse 5) and would "make war against the saints" (verse 7).

4. A beast represents a very powerful "kingdom" (see Daniel 7:23).

5. This beast will eventually have worldwide influence and control (verse 8).

6. This beast continues until the very end of time (Revelation 19:20).

It's true, this gigantic prophetic jigsaw puzzle does have a few other important pieces, but this is enough for now. So what are we looking for when it comes to this awesome and mysterious subject of the great Antichrist of Bible prophecy?

According to God's Holy Word, we are looking for an Antichrist that was starting to work in the time of Paul, but that was being restrained by the Roman Empire. It would rise up in the wake of a massive "falling away" from Jesus Christ occurring inside the Christian church and would be "revealed" after the Roman Empire fell in A.D. 476. It would be centered somewhere in Western Europe, would become self-exalting, and would even usurp the authority of God inside His own temple—that is, within Christianity. An actual "kingdom," it would have "eyes like the eyes of a man," being man-led and man-centered. It would make great claims for itself, having "a mouth speaking great things." It will become powerful, persecuting, and deadly—even making "war on the saints." After developing global influence, it will eventually exercise significant control over the United Nations—over all countries on planet Earth. It will continue throughout Christian history, until the very end of time, yet it will finally be destroyed by the sin-consuming brightness of the glory of our Lord Jesus Christ.

Is such an Antichrist here now? Hold onto your seats! You are about to discover irrefutable proof that for over four hundred years the unanimous testimony of Protestant scholars, historians, and Christians has been, "Most definitely!"

CHAPTER 9

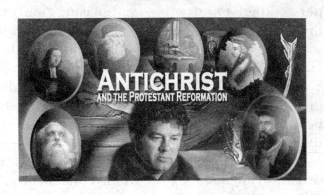

The New Testament church had an all-consuming desire to exalt Jesus Christ and His incomprehensible once-and-for-all sacrifice for the sins of the whole world (1 John 2:2; Hebrews 10:12). The book of Acts reports, CNN-style, how the message of Christ's grace spread like an uncontrollable brush fire all over the Roman Empire (Acts 2:36-41; 5:14; 8:4). As the apostles lifted up the crucified One before the multitudes, sinners realized *they were loved by God* in spite of their faults, and the Lord's power moved them to repent, to be baptized, and to stop serving Satan (Acts 2:38; 26:18). As the people trusted in Jesus Christ alone for salvation (Acts 16:31), He forgave their sins (Acts 13:38), transformed their hearts (Acts

15:8, 9), and set their feet on the path to Paradise.

As a result of the believers Spirit-filled preaching, strong churches were raised up in the midst of an idol-worshiping, pleasure-crazy, Caesar-devoted world. The new Christian converts were taught to obey the Bible above the traditions of men (Colossians. 2:8) and to cherish "every word that proceeds from the mouth of God" (Matthew 4:4). There was clearly seen to be only one way to the Father—Jesus Christ Himself (John 14:6), and Christians were taught to believe directly in Him (Ephesians 1:12), the Savior, the only Mediator between God and the human family (1 Timothy 2:5). They were also taught to *obey the truth* (1 Peter 1:22).

But as the Christian church rolled down the track of history, great changes soon took place. As Paul predicted, there came a tremendous "falling away" (2 Thessalonians 2:3) from the simplicity and purity of the gospel. Almost imperceptibly, false theories, man-made traditions, and unbiblical practices slipped into the very heart of Christianity. Little by little people lost sight of the beauty and love of Jesus. In the fourth century, during the time of Constantine, a large portion of the church compromised key Bible truths and decided to line up with the Roman state. As even more traditions came in, eventually Europe was wrapped in the Dark Ages.

By the time the 1500s came along, the original simplicity of the early Christian faith was almost unknown. All over Europe people were being taught to confess their sins to priests, to pray to the Virgin Mary, to buy "forgiveness notes" called indulgences, and to bow down to statues of the saints—none of which is taught in the New Testament. Monks even beat themselves in a misguided effort to earn the favor of God. It's true, there were sincere and godly people in what had become the Roman Catholic Church, but overall, Christianity was a mess! As Jesus Christ looked down from His throne, He probably told His angels, "It's time for the Protestant Reformation!"

Christians today should realize that it was *sincere Catholics* who wanted a change who originally spearheaded this Reformation. These Catholics initially had no thought of leaving the church of Rome; they simply wanted to redirect their Catholic countrymen away from the traditions of men and to lead them back to the pure truths of the Word. Their main goal was to lead other sinners like themselves away from trusting in their own works for salvation and into a simple faith in Jesus Christ. The Bible says, "Believe on the Lord Jesus Christ, and you will be saved" (Acts 16:31). "By grace you have been saved through faith, and that not of yourselves; it is the gift of God" (Ephesians 2:8). "Therefore having been justified [accepted] by faith, we have peace with God through our Lord Jesus Christ" (Romans 5:1).

Salvation is a wonderful *gift* from Jesus (Romans 6:23)! When we repent of our sins and receive this gift, trusting alone in Christ for salvation, the Father Himself will forgive our sins, change our lives, and give us power to obey the truth (Luke 13:3; 1 John 1:9; 1 Peter 1:22; John 17:17). This simple message of full and free salvation through what Jesus Christ has *already done* for us on the cross is called the Good News of the gospel (1 Corinthians 15:1-3). We must believe it fully, for it can save our souls (1 Peter 1:9).

Now let's get back to the topic of the Antichrist. The word "anti-Christ" literally means *against* or *in the place* of Christ, and in its most subtle manifestation it has to do with something that *claims loyalty to Jesus* while actually leading away from a pure faith in Him. Now let's connect this concept with what happened during the Reformation. As I have already said, the original Reformers were sincere Catholics whose only desire was to reform the church they loved from within. But as the fires of opposition heated up against them, they began to have serious doubts about the divine authority of that church itself. In other words, they began to question whether the Roman Catholic Church, as an institution centered in the popes and in the Vatican, was really the true church of Jesus Christ in the first place!

One by one the Reformers turned to the prophecies. In amazement they discovered what Paul had actually written about "the falling away," "the son of perdition," and a "mystery of lawlessness" that would proudly set itself up in the temple of God—which is the church (2 Thessalonians 2:3, 4, 7; 1 Corinthians 3:16). They were stunned to read Daniel's prophecy about a little horn with "eyes like the eyes of a man," "a mouth speaking great things," that would be centered in Western Europe, and that would make bloody "war against the saints" (Daniel 7:7, 8, 21). They shuddered as they realized this power was called "the beast" in God's last book, and that it would finally have worldwide influence and control (Revelation 13:2, 7, 8). As death sentence after death sentence was hurled against them for pointing sinners to Jesus Christ alone, and as the flames of the martyrs continued to blacken Europe's fair skies, these Reformers eventually came to a unanimous and solemn conclusion. They had discovered both Jesus Christ *and* Antichrist!

The following quotations are simply facts of history. The reader is encouraged to consider them squarely and honestly, in the light of Bible prophecy.

Martin Luther, Lutheran (1483-1546): "Martin Luther was the first to identify the papacy as such with the Antichrist. At first he discounted the value of John's Apocalypse. But then he saw in it a revelation of the Church of Rome as the deceiving Antichrist who secretly served Satan . . . a view that was to become dogma for all Protestant churches" (*Newsweek,* November 1, 1999. p. 71).

"Luther . . . proved, by the revelations of Daniel and St. John, by the epistles of St. Paul, St. Peter, and St. Jude, that the reign of Antichrist, predicted and described in the Bible, was the Papacy . . . And all the people did say, Amen! A holy terror seized their souls. It was Antichrist whom they beheld seated on the pontifical throne. This new idea, which derived greater strength from the prophetic descriptions launched forth by Luther into the midst of his contemporaries, inflicted the most terrible blow on Rome" (J. H. Merle D'aubigne, *History of the Reformation of the Sixteen Century,* book 6, chapter 12, p. 215).

On August 20, 1520, Luther declared, "We are of the conviction that the papacy is the seat of the true and real Antichrist" (Quoted in LeRoy Froom, *The Prophetic Faith of Our Fathers,* vol. 2, p. 121).

John Calvin, Presbyterian (1509-1564): "Daniel and Paul had predicted that Antichrist would sit in the temple of God. The head of that cursed and abominable kingdom, in the Western Church, we affirm to be the Pope" (*Institutes of the Christian Religion,* vol. 2, 1561 edition, pp. 314, 315).

"Some persons think us too severe and censorious when we call the Roman pontiff Antichrist. But those who are of this opinion do not consider that they bring the same charge of presumption against Paul himself, after whom we speak and whose language we adopt . . . I shall briefly show that [Paul's words in II Thess. 2] are not capable of any other interpretation than that which applies them to the Papacy" (*Ibid.* p. 410).

John Knox, Scotch Presbyterian (1505-1572): John Knox wrote about "that tyranny which the pope himself has for so many ages exercised over the church." Along with Martin Luther, Knox finally concluded that the papacy was "the very antichrist, and son of perdition, of whom Paul speaks" (*The Zurich Letters,* p. 199).

Thomas Cranmer, Anglican (1489-1556): "Whereof it followeth Rome to be the seat of antichrist, and the pope to be very antichrist himself. I could prove the same by many other scriptures, old writers, and strong reasons" (*Works by Cranmer,* vol. 1, pp. 6, 7).

Roger Williams, first Baptist pastor in America (1603-1683): Roger Williams spoke of the pope as "the pretended Vicar of Christ on earth, who sits as God over the Temple of God, exalting himself not only above all that is called God, but over the souls and consciences of all his vassals, yea over the Spirit of Christ, over the Holy Spirit, yea, and God himself . . . speaking against the God of heaven, thinking to change times and laws; but he is the son of perdition (II Thess. 2)" (Quoted in L. E. Froom,

The Prophetic Faith of Our Fathers, vol. 3, p. 52).

The Westminster Confession of Faith (1647): "There is no other head of the church but the Lord Jesus Christ. Nor can the pope of Rome in any sense be head thereof; but is that Antichrist, that man of sin and son of perdition that exalteth himself in the church against Christ and all that is called God" (Philip Schaff, *The Creeds of Christendom, With a History and Critical Notes,* vol. 3, p. 658, 659, chapter 25, sec. 6).

Cotton Mather, Congregational theologian (1663-1728): "The oracles of God foretold the rising of an Antichrist in the Christian Church: and in the Pope of Rome all the characteristics of that Antichrist are so marvelously answered that if any who read the Scriptures do not see it, there is a marvelous blindness upon them" (*The Fall of Babylon,* by Cotton Mather, quoted in L. E. Froom, *The Prophetic Faith of Our Fathers,* vol. 3, p. 113).

John Wesley, Methodist (1703-1791): Speaking of the papacy, John Wesley wrote, "He is in an emphatic sense, the Man of Sin, as he increases all manner of sin above measure. And he is, too, properly styled the Son of Perdition, as he has caused the death of numberless multitudes, both of his opposers and followers . . . He it is . . . that exalteth himself above all that is called God, or that is worshipped . . . claiming the highest power, and highest honor . . . claiming the prerogatives which belong to God alone" (*Antichrist and His Ten Kingdoms,* p. 110).

A great cloud of witnesses: "Wycliffe, Tyndale, Luther, Calvin, Cranmer; in the seventeenth century, Bunyan, the translators of the King James Bible and the men who published the Westminster and Baptist confessions of Faith; Sir Isaac Newton, Wesley, Whitfield, Jonathan Edwards; and more recently Spurgeon, Bishop J. C. Ryle and Dr. Martin Lloyd-Jones; these men among countless others, all saw the office of the Papacy as the antichrist" (Michael de Semlyen, *All Roads Lead to Rome,* p. 205).

The above quotes come from some of the most respected and influential Christians who have ever lived. They were sincere, intensely earnest, and honest men who based their conclusions on the prophecies of the Bible. I realize that times have changed. It's true, we are no longer in the Dark Ages; and yes, this is the twenty-first century. But there is something I want you to consider. Daniel's prophecy about a little horn (Daniel 7:8), John's prophecy about a beast having global influence (Revelation 13:2, 7, 8), and Paul's predictions about "the falling away" and the rise of an Antichrist that would sit in God's temple (2 Thessalonians 2:3, 4)—these prophecies are *still* in the Bible! And there is something else we must remember. Nations rise and fall; history rushes on; technology advances; and a new millennium has arrived—but God's Word has not changed!

CHAPTER 10

What time is it?" How many times have we heard that? The clock relentlessly governs our high-tech world. Cell phones, computers, night-stand radios, and spicy sports cars all have clocks in them. Clocks tell us when to get out of bed, when to leave for work, when it's time for lunch, and when to say, "Goodnight." In other words, we live our lives and make decisions based on *time.* This may surprise you, but even the Creator of the universe is concerned about time. His Book says, "When the fullness of *the time* had come, God sent forth His Son" (Galatians 4:4, italics supplied). The fact is that the entire life of Jesus was based on time. He knew when "His hour had come" (John 13:1) and when it was time for the supreme agony of His cross. Just as Jesus Christ's life was based on time, the same is true of the Antichrist. Paul predicted that after the Restrainer was removed, the Antichrist would "be revealed in *his own time*" (2 Thessalonians 2:6). What is the time of the Antichrist?

Daniel described the Antichrist as a little horn "making war against the saints, and prevailing against them" (Daniel 7:21). A few sentences later we read, "the saints shall be given into his hand for a time and times and half a time" (verse 25). *This is the time of the Antichrist.* This special time period is actually referred to seven times in God's Word, being spoken of as 3 1/2 times (Daniel 7:25; 12:7; Revelation 12:14), forty-two months (Revelation 11:2; 13:5), and 1,260 days (Revelation 11:3; 12:6). Most scholars realize that a "time" represents a year, and thus 3 1/2 times is the same as 3 1/2 years, or forty-two months, or 1,260 days. It's a matter of simple mathematics.

But is this a literal time period or a symbolic one? Consider this. Just as Daniel 7 reveals the time of the Antichrist (Daniel 7:25), even so does Daniel 9 reveal the time of Jesus Christ (Daniel 9:24). That latter prophecy pinpoints "seventy weeks" or 490 days. Almost all Bible scholars today interpret this 490-day period according to the day-for-a-year principle found in Ezekiel 4:6 and Numbers 14:34. Thus the 490 days are really *490 literal years.* We know this prophecy is a day-for-a-year because it begins with a command to rebuild Jerusalem after the Babylonian captivity (Daniel 9:25) and reaches all the way down to the first coming of Jesus Christ (Daniel 9:26). Because 490 literal days would not reach to the time of Jesus, the prophecy must be using a day-for-a-year. That's proof positive. Few question this.

Contemporary prophecy teachers of our generation definitely apply the day-for-a-year principle to the famous seventieth week of Daniel 9:27, which says, "Then he shall confirm the covenant with many for one week; But in the middle of the week He shall bring an end to sacrifice and offering" (Daniel 9:27). Based on the day-year principle, this "one week" is really *seven years.* Almost everyone agrees with this. Yet there is still a highly controversial dimension to this text. Many prophecy scholars today, as they interpret Daniel 9:27, have decided to sever this seventieth week from the first 69 weeks—and then after sliding it down to the end of time, they have decided to call it "the seven-year period of tribulation." According to this theory, the Rapture occurs at the beginning of the tribulation, and then the evil Antichrist will show up. But there is one major problem with this interpretation. Can you see it? Once again it puts the Rapture *before* the coming of the Antichrist! This should raise a major red flag in our minds.

Is there another sensible way of interpreting Daniel's seventieth week? Definitely! My book, *Exploding the Israel Deception,* lists ten reasons why it was really Jesus Christ who "confirmed the covenant with many" and who brought an end to the bloody "sacrifice and offering" by His death on the cross (see Matthew 26:28; Galatians 3:17; Romans 15:8; Hebrews 10:1, 2, 8, 12). Matthew Henry's famous Bible commentary, Adam Clarke's commentary, and the Jamieson, Fausset & Brown commentary all take this position.

The Protestant Reformers in the 1500s not only applied the day-for-a-year principle to Daniel 9:24-27 (the time of Jesus Christ), but also to the 3½ year period of Daniel 7:25 (the time of Antichrist). And they applied it to *Papal Rome*. Thus the 3½ years, forty-two months, or 1,260 days, all actually mean *1,260 literal years of papal rule*. Notice this quote from one of England's greatest Bible prophecy teachers:

> "The seventy weeks of Daniel, or 490 days to the Messiah, were fulfilled as 490 years; that is, they were fulfilled on the year-day scale. On this scale the forty-two months, or 1,260 days, are 1,260 years. We ask then, Has the Papacy endured this period? An examination of the facts of history will show that it has" (H. Grattan Guinness, *Romanism and the Reformation,* p. 84).

In 1701, Robert Fleming published his book, *The Rise and fall of Papal Rome.*

"Fleming showed, as others had done for many centuries, that the 1,260 days of prophecy represent 1,260 years" (*Ibid.* p. 156).

If you look closely, you will discover that Paul made a definite connection between the removal of the Restrainer and the time of the Antichrist. Notice carefully, "And now you know what is *restraining,* that he [the Antichrist] may be revealed in *his own time*" (2 Thessalonians 2:6). As we have already seen, this Restrainer was the fourth beast of Daniel 7—the Roman Empire. In A.D. 476, when Rome fell, the Restrainer was "taken out of the way." Thus we should expect the 1260-year period to begin *shortly after A.D. 476.*

H. Grattan Guinness does place the beginning of the 1,260-year period shortly after A.D. 476 He states that it began with "the notable decree of the emperor Justinian [A.D. 525-565] constituting the Bishop of Rome as the head of all Churches [in Western Europe]" *(Romanism and the Reformation,* p. 84). After the Roman Empire collapsed in A.D. 476, there were still rulers in the Eastern Empire. One, named Justinian, believed the key to peace in Europe was the uniting of all religions under the leadership of the Catholic Church. So he issued his famous decree which made the Pope the legal "Head of all the Holy Churches." This decree fully established the papacy's political power over all of Christianity in Western Europe. Justinian's decree went into effect in A.D. 538, which was shortly after A.D. 476! That key date—A.D. 538—marks the beginning of the time of the Antichrist.

Daniel predicted that during the 1260-year period the little horn would "persecute the saints of the Most High" (Daniel 7:25)—a prophecy that was fulfilled to the letter by papal Rome during the Dark Ages. By the end of this period, enough was enough, and Europe was ready for a change. If we start at A.D. 538 and count down 1260 years, this takes us to A.D. 1798—the time of the French Revolution. In a bloody reaction against the Roman Church for its horrendous history of persecution, Napoleon decided to abolish the papal government entirely. Can you guess what year this feat was accomplished? In 1798! That's why Mr. Guiness marks the conclusion of the 1260 years at the time of "the tremendous Papal overthrow in the French Revolution" (*Ibid.* p. 84).

In 1798, a general of Napoleon named Berthier entered Rome with a French army. He then swiftly abolished the papacy, dismissed the Vatican's Swiss guards, and proclaimed Rome to be a republic for France. "Berthier entered Rome on the 10th of February, 1798, and proclaimed a republic" (*The Modern Papacy,* p. 1, London: Catholic Truth Society). "One day the Pope was sitting on his throne in a chapel of the Vatican, surrounded by his cardinals. . . . Very soon a band of soldiers burst into the hall, who tore away from his finger his pontifical ring, and hurried him off, a prisoner" (*Epochs of the Papacy*, p. 449). Pope Pius VI was taken to France where he died in exile. "Napoleon gave orders that in the event of his death no successor should be elected to his office, and that the papacy should be discontinued" (*The Modern Papacy*, p. 1).

> The Papacy was extinct: not a vestige of its existence remained; and among all the Roman Catholic powers not a finger was stirred in its defense. The Eternal City had no longer prince or pontiff; its bishop was dying captive in foreign lands; and the decree was already announced that no successor would be allowed in his place (George Trevor, *Rome: From the Fall of the Western Empire*, p. 440).

This happened in the exact year 1798—marking the end of *the time of the Antichrist*. In that very year Protestant scholars all over Europe and America recognized the fulfillment of prophecy.

> In the downfall of the papal government . . . many saw in these events the accomplishment of prophecies, and the exhibition of signs promised in the most mystical parts of the Holy Scriptures (*History of France from 1790-1802*, vol. 2, p. 379).

Is not the *Papal power,* at Rome, which was once so terrible, and so domineering, at an end? But let us pause a little. Was not *this* End, in other parts of the Holy Prophecies, foretold to be, *at the* END *of* 1260 *years?*—And was it not foretold by Daniel, to be at the END of *a time, times, and half a time?* Which computation amounts to the same period. And now let us see; hear; and understand. THIS IS THE YEAR 1798 (Edward King, *Remarks on the Signs of the Times,* quoted by L. E. Froom, *The Prophetic Faith of Our Fathers,* vol. 2, p. 767).

Is it not extremely remarkable, and a powerful confirmation of the truth of *Scripture prophecy,* that just 1260 years ago from the present 1798, in the very beginning of the year 538, Belisarius put an end to the empire of the *Goths* at Rome, leaving no power therein but the *Bishop* of the *Metropolis?* Read these things in the *prophetic Scriptures;* compare them coolly with the present state of Europe, and . . . deny the truth of *Divine Revelation,* if you can. Open your eyes, and behold these things accomplishing in the face of the whole world. *This thing is not done in a corner.* (David Simpson, *A Plea for Religion and the Sacred Writings,* p. 166, quoted by L. E. Froom, *The Prophetic Faith of Our Fathers,* vol. 2, pp. 776, 777).

Remember, Paul wrote that after the Restrainer was removed, the Antichrist would "be revealed in his own time" (2 Thessalonians 2:6). Also remember Daniel's prediction that after the fourth beast fell, the little horn would rule for 1260 years—"making war against the saints" (Daniel 7:7, 8, 21, 25). In fulfillment of prophecy, shortly after Rome fell in A.D. 476, Justinian issued his famous decree giving the Roman Catholic Church total power in Europe. That decree went into effect in A.D. 538 Exactly 1260 years later, in 1798, Napoleon's general abolished the papacy's political power, thus ending that long and painful period of Papal rule—the time of the Antichrist.

But 1798 was not final end of the little horn. In a parallel prophecy we discover that the beast would go "into captivity" (Rev. 13:10). It would then receive its "deadly wound." Yet in words that have incredible meaning for us in the twenty-first century, God's final apocalyptic book declares, "His deadly wound was healed. And all the world marveled and followed the beast" (Revelation 13:3).

So what time is it? If you check your watch, computer, or cell phone, you can discover the exact minute in the Pacific, Mountain, Central or Eastern zones. But only the Bible reveals the time of both Jesus Christ *and* Antichrist.

According to God's clock, isn't it also time to believe in Jesus Christ, before it's too late?

CHAPTER 11

ANTICHRIST
AND JESUS CHRIST IN THE FLESH

Every time I travel overseas, I always carry my passport so I can identify myself before local or government officials. After comparing my face with my photo, they know it's me. In America, my driver's license serves the same purpose. It lists my name, birth date, height, hair color, and current address. These details are not so much for information, but for identification—that's the issue.

In addition to all the other puzzle-pieces we've looked at so far, the Bible gives another extremely important piece of information to help us identify that which is truly Antichrist. Notice carefully: "Every spirit that confesses that Jesus Christ has come in the flesh is of God, and every spirit that does not confess that Jesus Christ has come in the flesh is not of God. And this is that spirit of the Antichrist, which you have heard was coming, and is now already in the world" (1 John 4:2, 3). Again John wrote, "For many deceivers have gone out into the world who do not confess Jesus Christ as coming in the flesh. This is a deceiver and an antichrist" (2 John 7).

Thus the Bible plainly says twice that a denial that Jesus Christ has come in the flesh is a most definite mark of Antichrist. To use the analogy, if you ever wonder whether something or someone might be Antichrist, just look closely at the information on their doctrinal "passport"or "driver's license." If you see the words, "Doesn't confess that Jesus Christ has come in the flesh"—you have your answer.

Every Christian should "confess" that Jesus Christ has come in the flesh. But this confession must be more than a lips-only statement that Jesus Christ was a real person who was born of a virgin, lived a perfect life, and died on the cross. Amazingly, a person may confess all this and yet still be a "deceiver and an antichrist" (2 John 7)! According to the Bible, the confession must be more specific. We must confess that Jesus Christ is come in *the flesh*. And this confession must be genuine, from the heart, prompted by the Spirit of God (1 John 4:2). What does it really mean that "Jesus Christ is come in *the flesh*"? Let's delve deeper and find out.

The Bible says, "The Word became flesh, and dwelt among us" (John 1:14). "The Word" applies to Jesus Christ before He was born in Bethlehem. When "the Word became flesh"—it was then that the Infinite Son of God became a man. Now here's a key question, What *kind of flesh* did Jesus Christ become when He became a man? Notice carefully, "Forasmuch then as the children are partakers of flesh and blood, he also himself likewise took part of *the same*" (Hebrews 2:14, KJV). Don't miss it. The Bible says that Jesus Christ took "the same" flesh as "the children." "The children" doesn't apply to Adam and Eve, for they were never babies, but were created directly by God. Rather, "the children" applies to their descendants, that is, to *fallen humanity.*

Read it again, "As the *children* are partakers of *flesh* and blood, he also himself likewise took part of *the same*" (Heb. 2:14, italics supplied). Thus the Bible says that Jesus Christ "took" upon Himself the *same flesh* that we have. You might ask, "So what? What does this have to do with the Antichrist?"

First, we must understand what the "the flesh" is. "The flesh" is God's way of describing our basic, fallen human nature as it has been affected by sin. Paul said, "For I know that in me (that is, in my flesh) nothing good dwells" (Romans 7:18). In other words, the flesh is bad. It's our enemy.

It's like a nasty cesspool that often stinks and seeks to drag us down. "The flesh" is the channel through which Satan works to tempt us and lead us into sin.

One of the most awesome mysteries found in the Bible is the truth that "God was manifested in *the flesh*" (1 Timothy 3:16). It may be hard to fathom, but the fact is that Jesus Christ "took" upon Himself the very *same flesh* we have. Why did He do it? So that He could relate to us, understand our struggles, and reach us where we are. It also made it possible for Him to be tempted like we are. But there is one monumental truth we must never forget. Even though Christ took our flesh, He never sinned! He was "in all points tempted as we are, *yet without sin*" (Hebrews 4:15, italics supplied). Thus Jesus literally "condemned sin in the flesh" (Romans 8:3). Praise God! This means He took, met, and conquered the same flesh that gives us so much trouble!

Not only did Jesus defeat the flesh in our behalf, but He also died for *all* of our sins (1 Corinthians 15:3). Thus He is a perfect and complete Savior! After His total victory over Satan, Jesus ascended to heaven to become our great High Priest. Notice the following connection between Jesus Christ's being tempted in the flesh like we are *down here* and His present ability *up there* as our High Priest to help us in our struggles.

Seeing then that we have a great high priest, that is passed into the heavens, Jesus the Son of God, let us hold fast our profession [or confession]. For we have not a high priest which cannot be touched with the feeling of our infirmities; but was in all points tempted like as we are, yet without sin. Let us therefore come boldly unto the throne of grace, that we may obtain mercy, and find grace to help in time of need (Hebrews 4:14-16, KJV).

Fantastic! Jesus Christ is now our great High Priest in glory. Because He took our fallen flesh down here, and conquered it, we can now come to Him by faith for mercy, grace, and power. It's true! Today, at this very moment, we can come right to His throne—direct, boldly!

Michael Dell has made Dell Computer Corporation one of the fastest growing and most successful computer companies in the world. How did he do it? By his business model—Be Direct. Dell Computers are not found at Best Buy, Circuit City, or Comp-USA. The only way to get one is to go directly to Dell and order for yourself. The genius of the Dell model is that it bypasses the middleman, makes money, and saves you money. That's its secret. It's the same with Jesus Christ. Because He took our flesh, becoming one of us, we can—Be Direct. Today, as our High Priest, Jesus lovingly and earnestly invites us to come straight to His throne.

Hebrews 2:17, 18 also firmly connects the reality of Jesus Christ's "coming in the flesh" with His High Priestly ministry and with His present ability to save us from sin.

> Therefore in all things He had to be made like his brethren, that He might be a merciful and faithful High Priest in things pertaining to God . . . For in that He himself has suffered, being tempted, He is able to aid those who are tempted.

Once again the truth is established. Because Jesus Christ was *made like* us in the flesh and was tempted like we are, He is now fully able as our great High Priest to help us when we are tempted. His arms are open wide. Even though we are unworthy and foolish sinners, we can still "come boldly to the throne of grace." Friend, we need no other mediator. We can "Be Direct." *This is all part of our confession.*

It's time to tie this in with the subject of the Antichrist. As we have already seen, it was the teaching of the major Protestant Reformers in the 1500s that papal Rome is the "little horn" (Dan. 7:8), the "beast" (Revelation 13:1), and "the man of sin" (2 Thessalonians 2:3)—the great Antichrist of Bible prophecy. So here's the multi-billion dollar question: Does the Roman Church genuinely confess that "Jesus Christ is come in the flesh"? On the surface it may claim to do so, but let's take a closer look.

One of the official doctrines, or "confessions," of the Church of Rome is the Immaculate Conception. Contrary to what one might think, this does not refer to the birth of Jesus as a sinless baby, but rather to the conception of Mary, Jesus' mother, inside the womb of her own mother. This doctrine teaches that when Mary was conceived, she was miraculously preserved from all sin. Thus her nature was "immaculate," or sinless—and therefore *different* from the rest of us. In other words, according to papal teaching, Jesus' mother did not have exactly the same flesh and nature that we have! Now don't miss this. What is the implication of this? According to papal Rome's official statements, when Jesus Christ was born, He took *Mary's nature, not ours.* If you think about it, this is a denial that "Jesus Christ has come in the flesh" (1 John 4:3)!

Here's the proof:

This is what the dogma of the Immaculate Conception confesses, as Pope Pius IX proclaimed in 1854: The most Blessed Virgin Mary was, from the first moment of her conception, by a singular grace and privilege of almighty God and by virtue of the merits of Jesus Christ, Savior of the human race, preserved immune from all stain of original sin (*Catechism of the Catholic Church*, p. 124.)

As a consequence, according to the Roman Church, when Jesus Christ was born, He took *Mary's nature, not ours*. The famous Cardinal Gibbons said it this way:

> In other words we affirm that the Second Person of the Blessed Trinity . . . by being born of the Virgin, [took] to Himself, from her maternal womb, a human nature of *the same substance with hers* . . . a true human nature of the same substance with *her own* (Cardinal Gibbons, *The Faith of our Fathers*, p. 167, quoted in John A. O'Brien, *The Faith of Millions: The Credentials of the Catholic Church*, p. 441, (italics added).

This doctrine of the Immaculate Conception with its idea of the entrance of Jesus into Mary's nature, not ours, really removes Christ one gigantic step away from the rest of us. As a result of this dogma, and others, Rome doesn't teach sinners to "Be Direct" by going straight to our heavenly Father through His Son Jesus Christ for salvation. Instead, the Vatican encourages poor sinners to come to Jesus Christ *through* Mary, popes, priests, and saints—that is, through the mediation of the Roman Catholic Church itself. Even more than this, Rome declares that by virtue of Mary's immaculate conception and supposedly sinless life, she now has a "saving office" in addition to her Son. Through Mary's "manifold intercession," she is now our "Advocate, Helper, Benefactress, and Mediatrix" who can "bring us the gifts of eternal salvation" and "deliver our souls from death"! (*Catechism of the Catholic Church*, p. 252).

Thus, in her official teachings, in spite of appearances, the Roman Church really denies that "Jesus Christ has come in the flesh" (1 John 4:3), that is, in *"the same"* (Hebrews 2:14) flesh as the rest of us. No matter what she may claim, Rome's declaration that Mary is our "Advocate" and "Mediatrix" leads away from a simple and pure faith in Jesus Christ *alone,* and thus really "denies the Father and the Son" (1 John 2:22). God's Word says, "Every spirit that does not confess that Jesus Christ is come in *the flesh* is not of God. And this is the spirit of the Antichrist, which you have heard was coming, and is now already in the world (1 John 4:2, 3).

As I conclude this chapter, I want to ask you directly: Is your own flesh dragging you down? Are you struggling with tobacco, alcohol, pornography, appetite, bitterness, an evil temper, or pride? If so (and who isn't battling with the flesh in some way?), I have good news for you. Not only did God's Son die on the cross for all your sins (1 Corinthians 15:3) thus enabling Him to forgive you totally, but "Jesus Christ has come in *the flesh*" (1 John 4:2, italics supplied). Yes, He took *our flesh* and conquered it! And now, as our great High Priest, "He is also able to save to the uttermost those that come to God through him, seeing he always lives to make intercession for them" (Hebrews 7:25). Because Jesus Christ has come in the flesh, He *alone* is our Savior, Intercessor, and Mediator. He is our Priest—and we need no other! "There is one God, and *one mediator* between God and men, *the Man Christ Jesus*" (1 Timothy 2:5, italics supplied). So "Be Direct" and come right now to His "throne of grace" for mercy, forgiveness, and power.

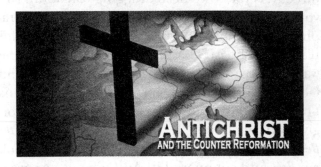

CHAPTER 12

T he Protestant Reformers of the 1500s had a major passion—to inspire sinners to "believe on the Lord Jesus Christ" (Acts 16:31) and to obey the Word of God above the traditions of men (Mark 7:13). But as they tried to lead their countrymen in Europe to the Bible alone, to Christ alone, to His grace alone, and to faith alone, they encountered fierce opposition from the Roman Church. As the persecution increased, it drove them deeper into their Bibles. Eventually, they turned to the prophecies. With special interest they pondered Paul's prediction about "the falling away," and a mysterious Antichrist taking his seat in "the temple of God" (2 Thessalonians 2:3, 4). They read about "the beast" (Revelation 13:1) and that "little horn"

with "eyes like the eyes of a man," and "a mouth speaking great things," who would "make war against the saints" (Daniel 7:8, 21). Finally, through the Holy Spirit's guidance, they put the pieces together and came to an amazing conclusion—they had discovered both Jesus Christ *and* Antichrist.

> "There are two great truths that stand out in the preaching that brought about the Protestant Reformation," American Bible commentator, Ralph Woodrow, reminds us, "The just shall live by faith, not by the works of Romanism and the Papacy is the Antichrist of Scripture." It was a message for Christ and against Antichrist. The entire Reformation rests upon this twofold testimony (Michael de Semlyen, *All Roads Lead to Rome,* pp. 202, 203).

John Wycliffe in England, Martin Luther in Germany, John Calvin in France, John Knox in Scotland, and Ulrich Zwingle in Switzerland, all preached that Jesus was *the Christ* and that the Roman papacy was *the Antichrist* of Scripture. As a result of this incredible, high-impact, double-edged message, the river of history changed its course. Hundreds of thousands of people left the Catholic Church.

As you can imagine, the Roman Church rose to its own defense in what has become known as the Counter Reformation. In 1545, she convened a special council destined to become the heart of her central intelligence operation against Martin Luther and the Protestants. This famous council took place north of Rome in a city called Trent. During its many sessions (which continued until 1563), the leaders of the Vatican developed a very sophisticated "game plan" to counteract the Reformers. Although this game plan included both the burning of Bibles and of heretics, it was decided that its most sophisticated aspect would be through *theology*. This is where the Jesuits come in.

On August 15, 1534, Ignatius of Loyola (1491-1556) founded the Society of Jesus, also called the Jesuits. "From the very outset of the Reformation, the Jesuit Order hung upon its heels as closely as its shadow" (Hagenbach, *op. cit.*, vol. 2, p. 404, quoted by L. E. Froom, *The Prophetic Faith of Our Fathers*, vol. 2, p. 466). This highly secretive and militant Catholic order definitely has a dark history of intrigue and sedition; that's why its members were expelled from Portugal (1759), France (1764), Spain (1767), Naples (1767), and Russia (1820). "Jesuit priests have been known throughout history as the most wicked political arm of the Roman Catholic Church. Edmond Paris, in his scholarly work, *The Secret History of the Jesuits,* reveals and documents much of this information" (Robert Caringola, *Seventy Weeks: The Historical Alternative,* p. 31).

The conflict between Romanism and Protestantism was basic and irreconcilable. The Romanist believed in the authority of the Church; the Protestant, in that of the Bible. The one yielded his conscience to the priest; the other, to God alone. The Romanist believed in the pope as the visible representative of Christ on earth; the Protestant looked, instead, upon the pope as Antichrist (Qeike, *op. cit.,* p. 484, quoted by L. E. Froom, *The Prophetic Faith of Our Fathers,* vol. 2, p. 471).

At the Council of Trent, the Catholic Church gave the Jesuits the specific assignment of counteracting Protestantism and bringing people back to the Mother Church. This was to be done not only through the Inquisition and through torture, *but especially through theology.* What kind of theology, you might ask? Here's the answer—by reinterpreting the prophecies about "the man of sin," the "little horn," and "the beast"!

Two very intelligent Spanish Jesuit priests rose to the challenge—Luis de Alcasar (1554-1613) and Francisco Ribera (1537-1591). In a nutshell, their strategy was one of reapplication and diversion, yet they went in opposite directions. Alcasar decided to apply the Bible's Antichrist prophecies *to the past,* to some ancient evil political ruler like Nero who lived in the first century. Meanwhile, Ribera applied these propheices *to the future,* to one supremely wicked "Mr. Sin" who would show up only at the very end of time. "Smart move!" declared the church. By reapplying the prophecies to the past and to the future, instead of to *the present,* these two Jesuit priests sought to divert the prophetic finger of truth thousands of miles away from the Vatican.

Notice these significant quotations:

> Accordingly, towards the close of the century of the Reformation, two of her [Rome's] most learned doctors set themselves to the task, each endeavoring by different means to accomplish the same end, namely, that of diverting men's minds from perceiving the fulfillment of the prophecies of the Antichrist in the Papal system. The Jesuit Alcasar devoted himself to bring into prominence the *Preterist* method of interpretation . . . to show the prophecies of Antichrist were fulfilled before the Popes ever ruled at Rome, and therefore could not apply to the Papacy. On the other hand the Jesuit Ribera tried to set aside the application of the prophecies to Papal Power by bringing out the *Futurist* system, which asserts that these prophecies refer properly not to the career of the Papacy, but to that of some future supernatural individual, who is yet to appear, and to

continue in power for three and a half years (Joseph Tanner, *Daniel and Revelation*, pp. 16, 17, quoted by L. E. Froom, *The Prophetic Faith of Our Fathers*, vol. 2, p. 487).

In 1590, Ribera published a commentary on the Revelation as a counter-interpretation to the prevailing view among Protestants which identified the Papacy with the Antichrist. Ribera applied all of Revelation but the earliest chapters to the end time rather than to the history of the Church. Antichrist would be a single evil person who would be received by the Jews and would rebuild Jerusalem (George Eldon Ladd, *The Blessed Hope: A Biblical Study of the Second Advent and the Rapture*, pp. 37-38).

Ribera denied the Protestant Scriptural Antichrist (2 Thess. 2) as seated in the church of God—asserted by Augustine, Jerome, Luther and many reformers. He set on an infidel Antichrist, outside the church of God (Ron Thompson, *Champions of Christianity in Search of Truth*, p. 89).

At the close of this chapter, I want to clarify these three important "isms"—Preterism, Futurism, and Historicism. Preterism is what Alcazar taught. Its root word is "pre," pointing back to the past. Preterism involves the belief that the Bible's Antichrist prophecies have all been fulfilled in the distant past in someone like Nero, who lived in the first century.

Futurism is what Ribera taught. Its core concept is that these prophecies apply to only one evil individual who will crash into history during time's last sliver.

In opposition to both Preterism and Futurism is Historicism, which, in this Christian context, has to do with historical progression. Historicism is the belief that the prophecies of Daniel and Revelation find fulfillment *throughout the history of Christianity*. It also places special emphasis on the on-going struggle between Jesus Christ and Satan *inside* the Christian church.

Historicism recognizes "the falling away" that Paul predicted. It also takes note of the rise and development of the Roman Catholic Church, which, although professedly a Christian institution, teaches doctrines which lead away from a pure and simple faith in Jesus Christ alone. Historicism was the prophetic prospective of all of the Protestant Reformers. While not wanting to attack sincere individuals, Historicism nevertheless points its finger at the Vatican, while both Preterism and Futurism reflect the razor-sharp counter-ideas of the Jesuits and the council of Trent's strategic game plan *to divert attention away from Rome*.

CHAPTER 13

THE PROTESTANT SWITCH
TO A NEW ANTICHRIST

Code Red, Melissa, Good Times, and Ripper—
what do they have in common? They are computer
viruses that can turn one's beloved laptop or PC into
a terribly malfunctioning machine that becomes
good for nothing. Just as Osama bin Laden has become Public Enemy Number #1 to the United States,
even so has the computer virus become Public Enemy #1 to all who sit in front of a monitor.

Computer viruses are very sophisticated and
destructive software programs designed by evil
people who take pleasure in hurting others. Tiny
technical terrorists, they can slip unnoticed into
your computer and ruin everything. The most
common way for a virus to get inside is via an attachment connected to an apparently friendly

email. You might get a message from a stranger that says, "Click here and look at my family photos!" As soon as you click on the attachment to view the pictures—it's too late. Once the virus is inside your computer it quickly multiplies itself like a malicious cancer cell. Often the virus starts removing data, deleting files, and messing everything up. Eventually your computer can totally crash, and if that happens, it's all over. You've lost everything. Time for a new computer.

This chapter is about prophecy, not computers, but we can still learn a big lesson from the computer virus. As we have already seen, the Protestant Reformers held two core beliefs: (1) Salvation is through Jesus Christ alone; and (2) Papal Rome is the Antichrist of Scripture. Their prophetic perspective was called Historicism. In the language of computers, we might say that Historicism was their basic prophetic operating system, much like Windows 98 and Windows 2000 are now the main operating systems for most Microsoft-based computers. Even though computer programs and systems become quickly outdated because of upgrades to better versions, it is an amazing fact that Historicism remained intact as the primary operating system of most Protestant Churches for almost 400 years! Have you heard the expression, "I'd rather fight than switch"? That's how most Protestants felt about Historicism from the 1500s all the way down to the early twentieth century.

But today in the twenty-first century, Historicism is out, and Futurism is in! What happened? How did the shift take place? The story is both fascinating and tragic. Here are some of the highlights. We have already seen that at the Council of Trent the Church of Rome reacted against the Reformation by commissioning the Jesuits to counteract the teaching of Historicism. In a short time the Jesuits Alcasar and Ribera put forth their theories. In this chapter, I am going to focus primarily on Ribera, because of the two his influence has become dominant.

Shortly after the Council of Trent, with the blessing of the pope, we might say that Fransicsco Ribera developed a virus—the virus of Futurism. For the next 300 years his Jesuit associates did their best to insert this virus into the Protestant churches, especially through educational processes connected with the universities of Europe, but they failed. Protestants were too smart and they consistently blocked its entrance. They basically said, "Sorry. We don't open attachments!"

The Futurism of Ribera never posed a positive threat to the Protestants for three centuries. It was virtually confined to the Roman Church. But early in the nineteenth century it sprang forth with vehemence and latched on to Protestants of the Established Church of England (Ron Thompson, *Champions of Christianity in Search of Truth,* p. 91).

Dr. Samuel Roffey Maitland (1792-1866), a lawyer and Bible scholar, became a librarian to the Archbishop of Canterbury. It is likely that one day he discovered Ribera's commentary in the library. In any event, in 1826 he published a widely read book attacking the Reformation and supporting the Jesuit idea of a future one-man Antichrist. For the next ten years, in tract after tract, he continued his anti-Reformation rhetoric. In the language of computers, we might say that inside Mr. Maitland's "readme text file," the virus lurked.

After Dr. Maitland came James H. Todd, professor of Hebrew at the University of Dublin. Giving credit to Maitland, Todd published his own futuristic pamphlets and books. Next came John Henry Newman (1801-1890), a member of the Church of England and a leader of the famous Oxford movement (1833-1845). In 1850, Newman wrote his "Letter on Anglican Difficulties" revealing that one of the goals in the Oxford movement was to eventually absorb "the various English denominations and parties" back into the Church of Rome. After publishing a pamphlet endorsing

Todd's futurism about a one-man Antichrist, Newman soon became a Roman Catholic, and later even a highly honored Cardinal. Through the influence of Maitland, Todd, Newman, and others, a definite "Romeward movement was already arising, destined to sweep away the old Protestant landmarks, as with a flood" (H. Grattan Guinness, *History Unveiling Prophecy or Time as an Interpreter*, p. 289). *The virus was coming in.*

Then came the Scottish Presbyterian minister Edward Irving (1792-1834), the acknowledged forerunner of both the Pentecostal and Charismatic movements. Irving pastored the large Chalcedonian Chapel in London with over 1,000 members. When Irving turned to the prophecies, he eventually accepted the one-man Antichrist idea of Todd, Maitland, Bellarmine, and Ribera, yet he went a step further. Somewhere around 1830, Edward Irving began to teach the rather unique idea of a two-phase return of Christ—the first phase being a secret rapture prior to the rise of the Antichrist. Where he got this idea is a matter of dispute. In his investigative books, journalist Dave MacPherson provides strong evidence that Irving accepted this new doctrine as a result of a prophetic revelation given to a young Scottish girl named Margaret McDonald. (See *The Incredible Cover-Up: Exposing the Origins of Rapture Theories,* by Dave MacPherson.) Regardless of where he got it, the fact is, Irving taught it!

In the midst of this growing anti-Protestant climate in England came John Nelson Darby (1800-1882). A brilliant lawyer, pastor, and theologian, Darby wrote more than fifty-three books on Bible subjects. On the positive side, he took a strong stand in favor of the infallibility of the Bible in contrast with the liberalism of his day. He became one of the leaders of a group called the Plymouth Brethren. Darby's contribution to the development of evangelical theology has been so great that he has been called The Father of Modern Dispensationalism. Yet John Nelson Darby, like Edward Irving, also became a strong promoter of a pre-tribulation Rapture followed by an end-time "Evil Individual"-type of Antichrist. In fact, this teaching has become a Dispensational pillar.

Dispensationalism is the theory that God deals with mankind in dispensations or periods. According to Darby, we are now in the "Church Age," that is, until the Rapture. After the Rapture, the seven-year period of Daniel 9:27 will supposedly kick in during which the Antichrist will purportedly rise up against the Jews. In fact, John Nelson Darby laid much of the foundation for the present popular removal of Daniel's seventieth week from history and from Jesus Christ in favor of applying it to a future tribulation after the Rapture. Thus Darby followed Irving, Todd, Maitland, and Ribera *by inserting the virus of Futurism into his theology.* He visited America six times between 1859-1874, preaching in all its major cities. As American Christians clicked "open" and received his messages, they had no idea that the virus was coming in, but that's what happened. Tragically, the Historicism of their forefathers was now being systematically moved toward the "Recycle Bin"—a computer term for the trash can.

One of the most important figures in this whole drama is Cyris Ingerson Scofield (1843-1921), a Kansas lawyer who was greatly influenced by the writings of Darby. In 1909, Scofield published the first edition of his famous Scofield Reference Bible. In the early 1900s, this Bible became so popular in American Protestant Bible schools that literally millions of copies were printed. What made these Bibles so popular was not so much the words of Scripture themselves, but the footnotes. And guess what? *Those footnotes contained the virus.* Interpretations were inserted that pointed the finger away from Papal Rome and toward a *future* Antichrist. As twentieth-century American Protestants taught others the ideas contained in Mr. Scofield's footnotes, the virus attacked file after file linked to Historicism—clicking "delete."

The Moody Bible Institute and the Dallas Theological Seminary have strongly supported the teachings of John Nelson Darby. Thus these Christian organizations, in spite of the good they have done and continue to do, have unknowingly enabled the virus to do what viruses do best—"multiply rapidly." Then in the 1970s, Pastor Hal Lindsey, a graduate of Dallas Theological Seminary, released his blockbuster book *The Late Great Planet Earth*. This 177-page, easy-to-read volume brought Futurism to the masses of American Christianity, and beyond. The *New York Times* labeled it "The number one best-seller of the decade." Over 30 million copies have been sold, and it has been translated into over thirty languages. Through *The Late Great Planet Earth* the Jesuit virus of Futurism made incredible progress in its intelligence strategy to replace Historicism as the prophetic operating system of the Protestant world.

Then came *Left Behind*. In the 1990s, Tim LaHaye and Jerry Jenkins took the future "Evil Man" idea of Hal Lindsey, Mr. Scofield, Darby, Irving, Todd, Maitland, and the Jesuit Ribera, and turned it into "The most successful Christian-fiction series ever" *(Publishers Weekly)*. The *Left Behind* books have been translated into many languages, have reached the best-seller lists of the *New York Times,* the *Wall Street Journal,* and *USA Today,* and are now being read by Christians of almost every denomination all over planet Earth. The central figure of this blockbuster series is Nicolae Carpathia—representing "Mr. Wicked" himself—that is, the future Antichrist. The result? The virus of Futurism has taken over, and Historicism has crashed!

The proper eschatological term for the view most taught today is Futurism . . . which fuels the confusion of Dispensationalism. The futuristic school of Bible prophecy came from the Roman Catholic Church, specifically her Jesuit theologians . . . However the alternative has been believed for centuries. It is known as Historicism (Robert Caringola, *Seventy Weeks: The Historical Alternative,* p. 6).

It is a matter for deep regret that those who hold and advocate the Futurist system at the present day, Protestants as they are for the most part, are thus really playing into the hands of Rome, and helping to screen the Papacy from detection as the Antichrist (Joseph Tanner, *Daniel and the Revelation: The Chart of Prophecy and Our Place In It, A Study of the Historical and Futurist Interpretation,* p. 16).

Before we finish this chapter, there is one more lesson we can learn from the virus. In May of 2001, a massive "Virus Alert" was sent out to computer users all over North America. The word was, "Beware of 'Sulfnbx.exe.' It's a virus that will become active on June 1. If you find it on your hard drive, delete it immediately before it ruins your computer!" As people looked deep inside their systems—behold, there was "Sulfnbx.exe"! Highly alarmed, yet thankful for the warning, many faithfully clicked "delete." But guess what? The whole thing was an evil scam! "Sulfnbx.exe" was not a virus after all, but is rather an original component of all Microsoft computers! Tricky virus makers had won again through a new strategy of convincing the public, in the name of safety, to delete something they really needed.

Can you see the lesson here? The virus of Futurism has now almost entirely replaced Historicism as the prophetic operating system in the Protestant world. But if that's not enough, Satan has another deception waiting in the wings. Are you ready for it? He is now trying to switch everything around by convincing sincere Bible-believing Christians that Historicism is really the virus, a new Public Enemy #1, that should be removed! "Delete Historicism.exe! It's divisive and dangerous!" *says Lucifer.*

Don't be fooled! The truth is, Historicism is not a newcomer, nor a virus, but is really part of the original operating system of one of the most powerful Christian movements in history—the Protestant Reformation!

It won't ruin your computer. You need it. It could save your life.

CHAPTER 14

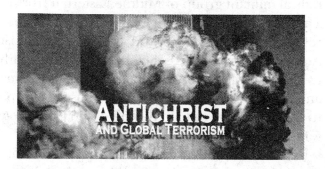

September 11, 2001 may go down in history as America's darkest day. Like thieves in the night, terrorist hijackers took over four U.S. planes, ramming two of them into the twin towers of the World Trade Center in New York City, and one into the Pentagon. I vividly remember, shortly after 9:00 A.M., watching my television set in horror as the second tower collapsed before my eyes—live! Oh what a wicked act of senseless cruelty! As I have read the stories in *Newsweek* of the families left behind, I have cried myself, wondering, "O God, how long?" Our nation may never fully recover from the shocking effects of that unspeakably terrible Tuesday morning.

As everyone knows, the suspected mastermind behind this "Attack on America" is Saudi-born

Osama bin Laden, one of the leaders of an ultra-radical militant group of Middle Eastern terrorists. The shocking reality is that Osama claims to be very religious, a follower of God; his hatred against America stems from his belief that our nation—with its VCRs and blue jeans—is the "Great Satan." Osama and his devotees are on a religious crusade to wipe us all out. They're calling this battle a Jihad, or "holy war," and are waging it in the name of God.

Osama bin Laden is not the only one who has ever mistakenly waged war against others in the name of God. It's been done before, and will probably be done again. Sadly, this kind of evil is often described in "the Scripture of Truth" (Daniel 10:21).

Jesus solemnly warned His disciples, "The time is coming that whoever kills you will think that he offers God service" (John 16:2). There it is—murder in the name of God. Historically, this has already happened among different religions and groups. But the focus of this book is the Antichrist. Just as global terrorists are now waging a "holy war" against the United States of America, the "Scripture of Truth" says the Antichrist will conduct a similar warfare against God's church.

The Little Horn: "I was watching; and the same horn was making war against the saints, and prevailing against them" (Daniel 7:21).

The Beast: "It was granted to him to make war with the saints and to overcome them. And authority was given him over every tribe, tongue, and nation" (Revelation 13:7).

The Harlot of Babylon: "I saw the woman, drunk with the blood of the saints and with the blood of the martyrs of Jesus" (Revelation 17:6).

These chilling words describe a definite war against God's saints, waged not by Osama bin Laden and his terrorist network, but by the great Antichrist of Bible prophecy. When most Christians read these passages today, they usually apply them to a *future* war to be waged by a *future* Antichrist against a group of *future* "tribulation saints" left behind after the Rapture. This is total Futurism! The virus at work again.

The truth is, hidden deep within the pages of history is a very real record of almost unspeakable horror, darkness, bloodshed, and persecution that has already been waged by the real beast of Bible prophecy. As with modern terrorists, it was also waged as a "holy war." The true details of this history, and its connection with prophecy, used to be understood by the majority of Protestants, that is, until *the switch* to a new Antichrist.

Before I go any further, I want to make a few points perfectly clear. There are millions of honest Muslims today who recoil at the acts of bin Laden. Obviously, these individuals are not responsible for the slaughter in New York City and Washington D.C. Likewise, millions who now belong to the Roman Catholic Church are not responsible for the past and should not be blamed for persecutions carried out in the name of religion. And we should not forget that many Protestants have cruelly persecuted Catholics, and for this they will be judged. As the horrible scenes from New York City remain in our minds, I appeal to all of my readers to respect human life, no matter what religion one chooses. Nevertheless, this book is about prophecy, and this "war against the saints" is a very definite part of God's Word.

Speaking about the little horn, the prophet Daniel said, "I was watching; and the same horn was making war against the saints, and prevailing against them" (Daniel 7:21). This passage has literally been fulfilled, and behind this text lies a nightmare too horrible to describe. If you so desire, you can read for yourself *Fox's Book of Martyrs* (by John Fox), *A Woman Rides the Beast* (by Dave Hunt), *History of the Waldenses* (by J. A. Wylie), *Vicars of Christ: The Dark Side of the Papacy* (by Peter de Rosa), *Heresy, Columbus and the Inquisition* (by Salim Japas), or the *History of the Inquisition* (by Jean Antoine Llorente). That is, if you have a strong stomach.

That the Church of Rome has shed more innocent blood than any other institution that has ever existed among mankind, will be questioned by no Protestant who has a complete knowledge of history (William E. H. Lecky, *History of the Rise and Influence of the Spirit of*

Rationalism in Europe, vol. II, p. 35).

The problem is, most Protestants have lost the knowledge of history!

The Holy Office of the Roman Catholic Inquisition was created for the express purpose of discovering, counteracting, and eliminating "heresy" from planet Earth. "Although we do not know exactly what year this infamous Office was founded, we can state that its origin came about during the pontificate of Gregory IX, between 1227 and 1233" (Salim Japas, *Heresy, Columbus and the Inquisition,* p. 1). Like a black cloud, it soon spread all over Europe and England, and later even as far as India and Mexico. The Roman Church has never officially abolished it. Instead, its name was changed in 1967 to the Congregation for the Doctrine of the Faith.

> Making every allowance required by a historian and permitted to a Christian, we must rank the Inquisition, along with the wars and persecutions of our time, as among the darkest blots on the record of mankind, revealing a ferocity unknown in any beast (Will Durant, *The Story of Civilization,* vol. 4, p. 784).

The story of the Inquisition is one of dark chambers, torture rooms, priests dressed in black, religious persecution, and pain. Many of its details are too morbid and horrifying to mention.

> Disregarding the maxims and the spirit of the Gospel, the papal Church, arming herself with the power of the sword, vexed the Church of God and wasted it for centuries, a period most appropriately termed in history, the "dark ages." The kings of the earth, gave their power to the "Beast." (*Fox's Book of Martyrs,* p. 43).

Thus the much-respected Christian classic, *Fox's Book of Martyrs,* applies Revelation's prophecy about "the Beast" to the Church of Rome rather than to some future "Mr. Evil." I realize that such a view is not "politically correct" today. It is much easier, safer, and less offensive to apply the prophecies of the beast and the little horn to some future personage like Nicolae Carpathia as described in the *Left Behind* series. Modern blockbuster books and high-tech movies that present this view may appeal to the masses, but we should ask: Are they true? When the twin towers of the World Trade Center collapsed, what happened? Americans were instantly jolted away from fantasy into the sober realities of a real world on the brink of a very real and deadly war. In such serious times as these, shouldn't Christians today also pull away from fictitious ideas about prophecy and *return to the truth*?

The Bible says the little horn will make war against the saints (Daniel 7:21). One respected Bible commentator has declared,

> Can anyone doubt this is true of the papacy? The Inquisition, the "persecutions of the Waldenses;" the ravages of the Duke of Alva; the fires of Smithfield; the tortures of Goa—indeed, the whole history of the papacy may be appealed to in proof that this is applicable to that power. If anything could have "worn out the saints of the Most High"—could have cut them off from the earth so that the evangelical religion would have become extinct, it would have been the persecutions of the papal power. In the year 1208, a crusade was proclaimed by Pope Innocent III against the Waldenses and Albigenses, in which a million men perished. From the beginning of the order of the Jesuits, in the year 1540, to 1580, nine hundred thousand were destroyed. One hundred and fifty thousand perished by the Inquisition in thirty years. In the Low Countries fifty thousand persons were hanged, beheaded, burned, and buried alive, for the crime of heresy, within the space of thirty-eight years from the edict of Charles V against Protestants, to the peace of Chateau

Cambreses in 1559. Eighteen thousand suffered by the hand of the executioner in the space of five years and a half during the administration of the Duke of Alva. Indeed, the slightest acquaintance with the history of the papacy will convince anyone that what is here said of "making war with the saints" (verse 21), and "wearing out the saints of the Most High" (verse 25), is strictly applicable to that power, and will accurately confirm its history (Albert Barnes, *Notes on Daniel,* p. 328.)

Dave Hunt is a best-selling evangelical author. In his controversial book, *A Woman Rides the Beast,* he appeals to contemporary Christians, "Try to imagine being suddenly arrested in the middle of the night and taken to an unknown location kept secret from family and friends. You are not told the charges against you nor the identity of your accusers, who remain unknown and thus immune from any examination to discover whether they are telling the truth. Whatever the accusation, it is accepted as fact and you are guilty without trial. The only 'trial' will be by the most ingeniously painful torture that continues until you confess to that unnamed crime of heresy of which you have been accused. Imagine the torment of dislocated joints, torn and seared flesh, internal injuries, broken bones on the rack and other devices, mended by doctors so they could be torn asunder by fresh torture. Eventually you would confess to anything to end the torment, but no matter what you confess it never fits the secret accusation, so the torture continues until at last you expire from the unbearable trauma.

"Such was the fate of *millions*. These were real people, mothers, fathers, brothers, sisters, sons, and daughters—all with hopes and dreams, with passions and feelings, and many with a faith that could not be broken by torture or fire. Remember that this terror, this evil of such proportions that it is unimaginable today, was carried on for *centuries* in the name of Christ by the command of those who claimed to be the vicars of Christ" (Dave Hunt, *A Woman Rides the Beast,* p. 250).

It's true, those people *back then* were just as real as those who perished in the Twin Towers, at the Pentagon, and in that fourth plane that crashed in Pennsylvania. As I have thought about the families and read the stories of September 11, my heart has been broken. One evening as my wife and I watched the news, we both cried. Later we just held each other, stunned. Terrorism has hit on the home front; now we know; now we feel; now we Americans understand what others have experienced.

Those whom Dave Hunt described have also suffered. But there is one major difference. On September 11, most died rather quickly, while those who felt the wrath of the Inquisition often agonized for days, even months! The ones in torture chambers had no cell phones. They couldn't call home to say, "I love you!" Thousands perished in the Twin Towers, yet *millions* lost their lives when the little horn "made war with the saints" (Daniel 7:21). This is not fictitious fantasy, but the fullness of a terrible reality.

God loves all who have died at the hands of terrorists, whether during the Dark Ages or just recently. And somehow, He even loves the terrorists themselves. When Jesus Christ died, He died for everyone, including Osama bin Laden. Of course there are lots of honest Muslims in the world, and Catholics, and Protestants, and Jews. Nevertheless, if there is one lesson September 11 should teach us all, it's this—there is no excuse for *religious murder in the name of God!* This applies to Muslim extremists, popes, Protestant and Jewish militants—to all of us. God says, " 'Vengeance is Mine; I will repay,' says the Lord" (Hebrews 10:30). When it comes to judging and executing sentence against evil, this is definitely not our work. If anyone disagrees, contrary to Hebrews 10:30, they will have to answer to the Almighty Himself on Judgment Day.

You have reached the end of *The Antichrist Chronicles,* but not the end of biblical prophecies. What does the future hold? My book, *Truth Left Behind* (see back pages for details) provides more "top secret intelligence information" from the Bible about Earth's final crisis, Antichrist's last move, the Mark of the Beast, Babylon, the seven last plagues, and the ultra-glorious return of Jesus Christ to take His children home. But "of these things we cannot now speak in detail" (Hebrews 9:5).

Steve Miller was inside the fully intact South Tower of the World Trade Center just minutes after the north tower burst into flames. As he and his associates descended from the eightieth floor, he paused on the fifty-fifth floor to use the men's room. It was a little after 9:00 am. "Should I phone my wife?" he pondered. Suddenly a voice was heard over the public-address system: "Don't panic. The building is safe. Return to your offices." As he glanced sideways at the flaming building next door and saw people jumping from windows a thousand feet above the ground, his distrust of official voices prevailed. He was heading for the stairs when a second plane exploded into the South Tower just a few floors above him. He got out, and as he hurried across the bridge toward Brooklyn, he looked back just in time to see his building vanish in a cloud of smoke. Upon his arrival at home his teary-eyed wife fell into his arms. "Oh, my God," she cried, "I thought you were dead."

My final advice to you is this: Don't trust every official-sounding voice you hear. There are times when we must go against the grain, in the opposite direction of the crowd. Sincere prophecy teachers who now advocate Preterism or Futurism may say, "Don't panic. Our theories are safe. Stay in the building." But the fact is, someday both towers of prophetic error will be totally vaporized.

What you have learned about the Antichrist *is true*. You have discovered what prophecy teachers aren't telling you. Before the final crisis comes, before the storm hits, before the Mark of the Beast bursts upon us like a terrorist attack on a crisp Tuesday morning, my appeal to you is this: Fall into the loving arms of Jesus Christ before it's too late.

Outside Jerusalem, on a hill called Calvary, Jesus Christ died for every Jew, Muslim, Christian, Protestant, Catholic, Hindu, Sikh, and atheist. His agony was for all Republicans and Democrats. He felt the horror of sin for every alcoholic, drug-addict, prostitute, and child-abuser. He even died for Osama bin Laden and his suicidal terrorist companions. But above all, He died for you! You may now come to Him—directly—without any other mediators. If you repent of your sins and trust Him fully, personally, Jesus will grant you the free gift of eternal life and save you by His grace (Romans 6:23).

I will close this book with these wonderful words that should give hope to us all: "I saw a new heaven and a new earth, for the first heaven and the first earth had passed away . . . And God will wipe away all tears from their eyes; and there shall be no more death, nor sorrow, nor crying. There shall be no more pain, for the former things have passed away" (Revelation 21:1, 4).

"Even so, come, Lord Jesus!" (Revelation 22:20).

(Video/DVD/Audio Album/Book pictured)

The Antichrist Chronicles (as seen on national television!) is now available on video, DVD, and in an audio album. Twelve half-hour programs contain stunning, original graphics and high-quality animations. The series is great for church services, prayer meetings, and for sharing with everyone!

Quantity discounts available for the book.

Orders only: 1.800.795.7171
(Visa/Master Card accepted)

Additional Resources
with Steve Wohlberg

Amazing Discoveries Bible Prophecy Seminar

24 programs explore the Bible's most important end-time prophecies. Subjects include: From Hollywood to Heaven (Steve's story), A Thief in the Night, 1,000 Years and the Lake of Fire, the 144,000, & much more!

Jewish Discoveries in Scripture

8 half-hour programs with six Jewish believers who discuss the Torah, the Ten Commandments, the Messiah, the Nazi Holocaust, and other sensitive Jewish/Christian issues. Great for sharing with your Jewish friends!

Orders only: 1.800.795.7171
(Visa/Master Card accepted)

or write:

Texas Media Center
PO Box 330489
Fort Worth, TX 76163
1.817.294.0053

www.truthleftbehind.com

* These resources are also available at ABC outlets nationwide.